ACTS OF THE CONGRESS

Rule – General Declarations - Proposal

III INTERNATIONAL CONGRESS

LAY DOMINICAN FRATERNITIES

FATIMA 2018

Acts of the Congress
Rule General Declarations Proposals

III International Congress of Lay Dominican Fraternities Fatima 2018

Edited by Edoardo Mattei

International Council
Lay Dominican Fraternities

ISBN: 9781095196922

Published by
Intenational Council of Lay Dominican Fraternities (ICLDF)
Piazza Pietro d'Illiria 1
00100 – Roma
publisher@fraternitiesop.com

Article 34.4
Men and Women in Mission Together

*Lay men and women offer a unique
vision of preaching and living the
Gospel because of their total insertion
into society with all of its secular,
economic, and political realities. They
are able to live shoulder to shoulder
with men and women with whom our
religious brothers and sisters will
hardly have contact. The friars and
sisters need their vision and expertise.*

ACTS GENERAL CHAPTER – BOLOGNA 1998

Introduction

This book contains the official documentation published following the III International Assembly of Lay Dominican Fraternities as important as a General Chapter.

It is not in testimony of a historical event for participation and results, but a working tool both for the Provincial Councils, in their work on updating the National and Provincial Directories, and for the Dominican Laity, who should be interested in the progress of lifestyle .

For this reason, the structure of the book does not comply with the chronology of events. It is a guide-like arrangement, starting with the Approval Decrees then changes to the Rule and the General Declarations.

After this first part dedicated to the documents of the Curia, it provides Proposals (only those approved and not in opposition to the Rule or the Constitutions) that will have to be in account while updating of the DIrectories.

Finally, the official texts of the main speeches held during the Fatima Assembly are published. In this regard, the translation work has encountered the typical problems: translating literally or according to the content? It was chosen a literal translation closest to the spirit of the Assembly which wanted to highlight the cultural values of each country. In this way, styles and idioms are unchanged preserving the freshness and peculiarity original, perhaps to the detriment of the understanding.

Finally, I would like to thank Ruth Anne Henderson for her tireless help in translations and for her availability and friendship.

A special mention to fr. Rui Lopes op, general promoter of the laity, for his devotion to the laity and honoring me with his friendship.

Edoardo Mattei
Social Media Manager "Fraternities OP"

RULE

GENERAL

DECLARATIONS

Rule and General Declarations

PRINCIPLES

Dear friends,

Here are some indications regarding the legislation which has reached you. First and foremost, I ask the members of the ICLDF to communicate it as quickly as possible to their regions.

I have delivered the document to you as signed by the Master of the Order. The original of the document was written in English (apart from the text of the Rule) and you must always refer to that text if you find something difficult to interpret.

Don't worry if you find the text of the Rule in Latin. It is the same Rule as you already have, apart from

> n° 20 c): A Provincial President and a Provincial Council of Lay Dominicans is to be elected by the fraternities, in accordance with the norms of their particular directory. This council will elect the Provincial President of the Laity; and

> 21 b): The president and the council of the fraternity are elected for a set time and in accordance with the manner established by the particular directory.

When you print the text of the Rule, do not forget to publish the decree of approval dated 1987, which you already know, signed by Cardinal Hammer, the text of the Master of the Order Damian Byrne, and the text of the Congregation for Institutes of Consecrated Life and Societies of Apostolic Life, which approves changes to the Rule and which I also send you at this time.

The declarations form a new body: from now on the preceding declarations will not be published, having been abrogated by the new declarations; as you see they are separated by titles which will help you when you consult them. I want to remind you that the provincial directories must be in agreement with the Rule and the Declarations: please revise the Directories to bring them up to date.

I wish to draw your attention to a certain number of points:

- **n° 4** which tells us that if anyone wants to make statements or anything of the sort in the press, on the Internet etc., in the name of the lay Fraternities, s/he must have the authorisation of the competent authority, defined by the Directories.
- **n° 6 § II** which tells us how far we can go for the integration of members of the IDYM, limiting it, always at the discretion of the Council of the Fraternity, to being flexible in the stages leading to one year of temporary promise.
- **n° 10** tells us how to go about making a directory: it must be done by the Lay Provincial Council, then proposed to the Prior Provincial and his council who must propose it to the Master of the Order with their opinion for his approval. If he considers it opportune, the Master of the Order may make amendments and after he has given his approval, the text will be sent to the Prior Provincial for him to promulgate it.
- **n° 16 §§** I and II indicate who may be religious assistant of

a Fraternity and what to do if s/he is not under the jurisdiction of the Prior Provincial.

- n° **18 §§ I, II and III** speak of the Provincial Promoter: the text is new and tells us that the Provincial Promoter is appointed for four years and can serve not more than two consecutive mandates.
- n° **19** provides us with a guide for the elections and how they should be carried out.

Please work on these points in the Fraternities. I remind you that **these norms come into force on 24 May 2019**.

I want to thank again the group who have helped me in this work: Edoardo Mattei, Ruth Anne Henderson, Bénédicte Jerebzoff and Maro Botica. Thank you so very much.

Finally, thanks to the Procurator of the Order and the Master of the Order for their invaluable support and collaboration, which made it possible to have these norms.

Fr. Rui Carlos Antunes e Almeida Lopes
op
General Promoter of Laity

CONGREGATION FOR RELIGIOUS
AND SECULAR INSTITUTES

Prot. No. D. 37-1 / 78

DECREE

The Master General of the Order of [Friars] Preachers on March 14, 1986 through the Procurator General, sent this Congregation the text of the *Rule of the Lay Fraternities of Saint Dominic* in order to obtain a definitive approval of this text.

After mature consideration, and with the favorable vote of the [Montreal] Assembly, this Congregation by the present decree approves the *Rule of the Lay Fraternities of Saint Dominic*, according to the Latin text, together with the corrections of the Assembly presented in the attached letter. A copy is being kept in the Congregation's Archives.

Anything to the contrary notwithstanding.

Given at Rome on January 15, 1987.

fr. Jerome Cardinal Hamer,
O.P.
Prefect

Archbishop Vincent Fagiolo
Secretary

**FRATRES ORDINIS PRÆDICATORUM
CURIA GENERALITIA**

To the Lay Fraternities of Saint Dominic:

Dear Brothers and Sisters in the Lord and Dominic:

Joyfully I give you the text of the Rule of the Lay Fraternities of Saint Dominic, which has very recently (January 15, 1987) been definitively approved by the Congregation for Religious and Secular Institutes.

The text of the former rule, promulgated by Fr. Aniceto Fernandez in 1969, was approved by the Holy See only on an experimental basis in 1972. The General Chapter held in Rome in 1983 commissioned the Master of the Order to hold an international meeting of the lay fraternities in order to renew and adapt the rule of the lay fraternities. This meeting, held in Montreal, Canada, June 24-29, 1985, produced the text which is now definitively approved.

Let this rule be in your hearts and in your fraternities as a gospel leaven to foster holiness and promote the apostolate together with the whole Dominican Family.

Greetings in the Lord.

Given at Rome, January 28, 1987,
on the feast of Saint Thomas Aquinas.

fr. Damian Byrne, O.P.
Master of the Order

fr. J. Martin, OP
Secretary   Prot. 50/86/87

CONGREGATIO
PRO INSTITUTIS VITAE CONSECRATAE
ET SOCIETATIBUS VITAE APOSTOLICAE

Ricev 15.02.19
73/18/777_Rules
MO MAR BE ORA →RCL

Prot. n. D. 37·1/96

BEATISSIMO PADRE

    Il Maestro Generale dell'*Ordine dei Predicatori* chiede a Vostra Santità la modifica dei nn. 20. (c) e 21 (b) della *Regula Fraternitarum Laicalium Sancti Dominici*, per le ragioni esposte.

    Questa Congregazione per gli Istituti di vita consacrata e le Società di vita apostolica, esaminata attentamente ogni cosa, approva le modifiche proposte, secondo il testo in lingua latina conservato nei suoi Archivi, dovendosi per il resto osservare quanto per diritto si deve osservare.

    Nonostante qualsiasi disposizione contraria.

    Dal Vaticano 28 gennaio 2019.

                    ✠ José Rodríguez Carballo, O.F.M.
                      Arcivescovo Segretario

Sr. Carmen Ros, NSC.
Sottosegretario

NOS
FR. BRUNO CADORÉ OP
TOTIUS ORDINIS PRÆDICATORUM
HUMILIS MAGISTER ET SERVUS

RULE OF THE LAY FRATERNITIES OF ST DOMINIC AND GENERAL DECLARATIONS

More than thirty years have passed since the from the definitive approval of the new Rule of the Lay Fraternities of St Dominic by the Sacred Congregation for Religious and Secular Institutes on 15 January 1987 (Prot. n. D. 27-1-87), and its promulgation by the Master of the Order, fr. Damian BYRNE, on 28 January 1987.

The Rule was complemented by a series of General Declarations promulgated by fr. Damian BYRNE on 16 February 1987 and various interventions of General Chapters and Masters of the Order in the following decades. Most notable are the General Declarations promulgated by fr. Carlos Alfonso AZPIROZ COSTA on 15 November 2007 following the International Congress of the Lay Fraternities of St Dominic at Buenos Aires in March of that year.

With the passage of time it has become apparent both to the International Council of the Lay Dominican Fraternities and to the International Congress of the Lay Fraternities meeting in Fatima in October 2018 that some minor adjustments to the Rule are necessary, along with some further clarifications in order to respond to the needs of the Fraternities across the world.

Therefore, having heard the International Council and Congress of the Lay Fraternities;

And having received the approval of the Congregation for Institutes of Consecrated Life and Societies of Apostolic Life on 28 January 2019 (Prot. n. D. 37-1/96) for amendments to nos. 20(c) and 21(b) of the Rule;

WE HEREBY PROMULGATE the following revised text of the Rule of the Lay Fraternities of St Dominic.

At the same time WE PROMULGATE the following revised General Declarations of the Master of the Order.

The new General Declarations integrally re-order the material of those made by our predecessors fr. Damian Byne on 16 February 1987 and fr. Carlos Alfonso Azpiroz Costa on 15 November 2007, and so those former Declarations are to be considered abrogated in accordance with canon 20.

The amendments to the Rule and the new General Declarations come into force on 24 May 2019, memoria of the Translation of Our Holy Father Dominic.

Given in Rome, at our General Curia at Santa Sabina, on 9 March 2019.

fr. Bruno Cadoré OP
Magister Ordinis

fr. Jean-Ariel Bauza-Salinas OP
Secretarius Generalis

Prot. n. 73/19/007 Rule

REGULA FRATERNITATUM LAICALIUM SANCTI DOMINICI

(NB. Titulus "fraternitates laicales" exprimi potest modo diverso ad mentem linguarum diversarum)

I. CONSTITUTIO FUNDAMENTALIS LAICATUS DOMINICANI

De laicis in Ecclesia

1. — Inter Christi discipulos, viri et mulieres in sæculo degentes, virtute Baptismatis et confirmationis, muneris prophetici, sacerdotalis et regalis Domini nostri Iesu Christi participes facti sunt. Ad hoc vocantur ut Christi præsentiam in medio populorum vividam reddant et "divinum salutis nuntium ab universis hominibus ubique terrarum cognoscatur et accipiatur" (Apost. Act. 4, 3).

De laicatu dominicano

2. — Aliqui vero, Spiritus Sancti motione ducti ad vitam secundum sancti Dominici spiritum et carisma adimplendam, Ordini incorporantur speciali promissione, secundum statuta ipsis propria.

De Dominicana Familia

3. — In communitatibus coadunantur et cum aliis coetibus Ordinis unam familiam constituunt (cf. LCO, 141).

• De specifico caractere laicatus dominicani

4. — Peculiari proinde modo signantur tum in propria vita spirituali, cum in servitio Dei et proximi in Ecclesia. Ut membra Ordinis, eius missionem apostolicam participant, studio, oratione et prædicatione secundum propriam laicorum conditionem.

De missione apostolica

5. — Ad exemplum S. Dominici, S. Catharinæ Senensis et maiorum nostrorum qui vitam Ordinis et Ecclesiæ illustraverunt, ipsi communione fraterna roborati, in primis de propria fide testimonium reddunt, hominum huius temporis necessitates audiunt et veritati serviunt.

6. — Apostolatus Ecclesiæ hodierni fines præcipuos sedulo considerant, speciali modo impulsi ad misericordiam veram erga omnes anxietates manifestandam, ad libertatem propugnandam, ad iustitiam et pacem promovendam.

7. — Charismate Ordinis inspirati, memores sunt apostolicam actionem ex abundantia contemplationis procedere.

II. De vita fraternitatum

De vita fraternitatum

8. — In vera communione fraterna ad mentem beatitudinum pro viribus vivant, quam etiam in qualibet circumstantia exprimant opera misericordiæ exercendo et quæ sua sunt impertiendo inter sodales fraternitatum, pauperes præsertim et infirmos; suffragia pro defunctis offerendo; ita ut omnibus sit semper cor unum et anima una in Deo (Act., 4, 32).

9. — Cum fratribus et sororibus Ordinis in apostolatu partem capientes, sodales fraternitatum vitam Ecclesiæ actuose participent, semper parati ut operam dent cum aliis consociationibus apostolicis.

10. — Fontes præcipui e quibus laici S. Dominici vires hauriunt ad proficiendum in propria vocatione, quæ coniunctissime contemplativa est simul et apostolica, hi sunt:

a) Divini verbi auscultatio et sacræ Scripturæ lectio, præsertim Novi Testamenti.

b) Quotidiana, quatenus possibilis sit, celebratio liturgica et sacrificii eucharistici participatio.

c) Reconciliationis sacramentum frequens celebratio.

d) Liturgiæ horarum celebratio una cum universa Familia Dominicana, necnon oratio in privato, sicut meditatio et mariale rosarium.

e) Conversio cordis iuxta spiritum et praxim pænitentiæ evangelicæ.

f) Studium assiduum veritatis revelatæ et constans cogitatio de problematibus huius temporis sub lumine fidei.

g) Devotio erga beatam Virginem Mariam, secundum traditionem Ordinis, erga sanctum Dominicum patrem nostrum et sanctam Catharinam Senensem.

h) Spirituales recollectiones periodicæ.

De formatione

11. — Dominicanæ formationis propositum est veros adultos in fide præbere ita ut apti sint ad verbum Dei accipiendum, celebrandum et proclamandum.

Cuique Provinciæ competit rationem conficere:

a) sive formationis progressivæ pro incipientibus.

b) sive formationis permanentis pro omnibus, etiam pro separatis membris.

12. — Quilibet dominicanus aptus esse debet ad verbum Dei prædicandum. In hac prædicatione exercetur munus propheticum christiani baptizati et Sacramento Confirmationis roborati.

In mundo hodierno verbi Dei prædicatio modo speciali sese extendere debet ad humanæ personæ dignitatem simulque vitam atque familiam propugnandam. Christianorum unitatem simul ac dialogum cum non christianis et non credentibus promovere ad dominicam vocationem pertinet.

13. — Fontes præcipui ad dominicanam formationem perficiendam hi sunt:

a) Verbum Dei et theologica cogitatio.

b) Oratio liturgica.

c) Historia et traditio Ordinis.

d) Documenta recentiora Ecclesiæ et Ordinis.

e) Scientia signorum temporum.

Professio seu promissio

14. — Ut Ordini incorporentur, sodales tenentur professionem emittere, seu promissionem qua formaliter promittunt secundum spiritum S. Dominici et modum vivendi a Regula præscriptum vitam ducere. Professio vel promissio ad tempus est aut perpetua. In professione emittenda sequens aut similis quoad substantiam formula adhibeatur:

«Ad honorem Dei omnipotentis Patris et Filii et Spiritus Sancti, et Beatæ Mariæ Virginis et S. Dominici, ego N.N., coram vobis N.N., priore (præsidente) huius fraternitatis et N.N., adsistente, vice Magistri Ordinis Fratrum Prædicatorum, promitto me velle vivere secundum Regular Laicorum S. Dominici (per triennium) (per totam vitam)».

III. DE STRUCTURA ET REGIMINE FRATERNITATUM

15. — Fraternitas est medium idoneum ad dedicationem cuiuscumque in propria vocatione nutriendam et augendam. Periodicitas coadunationum diversa est secundum fraternitates. Assiduitas cuiusvis sodalis propriam fidelitatem demonstrat.

16. — Candidatorum admissio, servatis dispositionibus a Directorio præscriptis quantum ad conditionem personarum et tempus admissionis, committitur responsabili laicali qui (quæ) præhabita votatione decisiva consilii fraternitatis, ad receptionem candidati, ritu a Directorio determinato, cum adsistente religioso, procedit.

17. — Post tempus probationis a Directorio determinatum et accedente voto Consilii fraternitatis, responsabilis laicalis accipit, simul cum adsistente religioso, professionem ad tempus vel perpetuam.

De iurisdictione Ordinis et fraternitatum autonomia

18. — Fraternitates laicorum subsunt iurisdictioni Ordinis; illa tamen autonomia gaudent, laicis propria, qua seipsas gubernent.

In universo Ordine

19. — a) Magister Ordinis, qua S. Dominici successor et totius familiæ dominicanæ caput, præest omnibus fraternitatibus in mundo. Ipsi competit integrum spiritum Ordinis in illis servare, normas statuere practicas pro opportunitate temporum et locorum et promovere bonum spirituale et zelum apostolicum sodalium

b) Promotor generalis vices gerit Magistri Ordinis pro omnibus fraternitatibus, quorum vota præsentat Magistro vel Capitulo Generali.

In Provinciis

20. — a) Prior provincialis præest fraternitatibus intra limites territorii suæ provinciæ ac, de consensu Ordinarii loci, novas fraternitates erigit.

b) Promotor provincialis (frater aut soror) vices gerit prioris provincialis et pleno iure participat Consilium provinciale laicorum.

Ipse nominatur a Capitulo provinciali vel a priore provinciali cum suo consilio, audito prius Consilio provinciali laicorum S. Dominici.

c) In territorio Provinciæ habeantur Præses provincialis et Consilium provinciale laicorum, electi a fraternitatibus et regulati iuxta normas a Directorio definitas.

In fraternitatibus

21. — a) Fraternitas localis gubernatur a præside cum suo consilio, qui plenam responsabilitatem moderationis et

27

administrationis assumunt.

b) Præses et Consilium eliguntur ad tempus et secundum modum a Directoriis particularibus statutum.

c) Adsistens religiosus (frater aut soror) adiuvat sodales in materia doctrinali et vita spirituali. Ipse nominatur a priore provinciali, auditis prius promotore provinciali et Consilio locali laicorum.

De Consilio nationali et internationali

22. — a) Ubi adsunt plures Ordinis provinciæ in eodem ambitu nationali, institui potest Consilium nationale, secundum normas a Directoriis particularibus statutas.

b) Simili modo exstare potest Consilium internationale, si tamen opportunum videatur, consultatis fraternitatibus totius Ordinis.

23. — Consilia fraternitatum vota et petitiones ad Capitulum provinciale fratrum Prædicatorum mittere possunt; Consilia provincialia et nationalia vero ad Capitulum Generale. Ad ista capitula aliqui responsabiles fraternitatum libenter invitentur ad materias tractandas quæ laicos spectant.

- Statuta fraternitatum

24. — Statuta propria fraternitatum laicalium sancti Dominici sunt:

a) Regula fraternitatum (Constitutio fundamentalis laicatus OP, normæ vitæ et regimen fraternitatum)

b) Declarationes generales, seu Magistri Ordinis, seu Capituli Generalis.

c) Directoria particularia

GENERAL DECLARATIONS

The Lay Fraternities of St Dominic

1. — § I – The Laity of St Dominic are those faithful who, baptised in the Catholic Church or received into her, confirmed and in full communion of faith, sacraments and ecclesiastical governance, are called by a special vocation to progress in the Christian way of life and to animate temporal things through the charism of St Dominic.

§ II – To be *incorporated* into the Order of Preachers in whose apostolic mission they fully participate, the Laity of St Dominic make the *promise* according to the formula foreseen by the Rule. Entry to the lay branch of the Order, called the *Lay Fraternities of St Dominic*, subject to the Master and the other Major Superiors of the Order, is brought about only with this promise.[1]

Other groups of Dominican Laity

2. — § I – In addition to the Lay Fraternities of St Dominic, there are Priestly Fraternities and other Associations and Confraternities, governed by their own Statutes legitimately approved by the competent authority and by various titles *attached* to the Dominican Family.

§ II – These Associations and Fraternities constitute a great and varied richness for the Church and the Dominican Family, and are to be greatly valued by all the members of the Lay Fraternities.

§ III – The formula of the promise contained in the *Rule of the Lay Fraternities of St Dominic* approved by the Holy See is not to be used by other groups aggregated in any way to the Dominican

---

1 C.A. AZPIROZ COSTA, *Dichiarazioni Generali circa la Regola della Fraternite Laiche di S. Domenico,* 15-xi-2007 (hereinafter DG2007), I § 1. These footnotes do not form part of the promulgated General Declarations, but are to indicate the source of each declaration.

Family, unless the Master of the Order expressly permits otherwise.[2]

Life of the Fraternities

3. — The Rosary, by which the mind is raised up to the intimate contemplation of the mysteries of Christ through the Blessed Virgin Mary, is a traditional devotion of the Order; therefore its daily recitation by the brothers and sisters of the Lay Fraternities of St Dominic is recommended.[3]

Apostolate of the Fraternities

4. — Members of the Fraternities are always to bear authentic witness to the mercy of Christ, in communion with the Church and the Order (cf. *Rule,* 5–7). To make public statements in the name of a Fraternity, or of the Dominican Laity more broadly, they require the authorisation of the competent authority in accordance with the Directory.

Admission to the Fraternities

5. — The Laity of St Dominic are always ascribed to a Fraternity, where possible that of their own canonical domicile or quasi-domicile, or are at least placed in stable contact with a member of the provincial or vicariate Council of the laity.[4]

6. — § I. – The perpetual promise is preceded by at least one year of initial reception and by three years of temporary promise, documented in the registers kept for this purpose either by the local Fraternity or in the provincial archive.[5]

§ II. – A candidate who has received an equivalent formation in the International Dominican Youth Movement may be dispensed

---

2 D. BYRNE, *Declarationes generales regulæ fraternitatum laicalium Sancti Dominici*, 16-ii-1987 (hereinafter DG1987), 5; DG2007, I § 2.

3 DG1987, 7.

4 DG2007, I § 3.

5 DG2007, I § 1.

from part of initial formation by the President of the Fraternity with the consent of the Council. In this case, at least one year of temporary promise is to precede perpetual promise.[6]

7. — The faithful who live in particular situations because of which in the judgement of the Council of the Fraternity it is not prudent that they be admitted to the promise may nevertheless participate in the life of the Fraternity and its permanent formation, in a path of following Christ through the Dominican charism, without prejudice to the discipline and Magisterium of the Church.[7]

The Law governing the Fraternities

8. — § I – The Rule by which the Lay Fraternities of St Dominic are governed is the fundamental law for the Lay Fraternities of the whole world.

§ II – The present General Declarations promulgated by the Master of the Order are expansions, explanations and interpretations of the Rule.

§ III – The Provincial and National Directories, prepared by the Fraternities themselves and approved by the Master of the Order, are particular norms for the local fraternities and for their collaboration at provincial and national level.[8]

9. — So that the brothers and sisters of the Lay Fraternities may fulfil their obligations "not as slaves under the law, but constituted as free people under grace" (St Augustine, *Rule*, 8; cf. Romans 6:14), we declare that transgressions against the Rule do not as such constitute moral fault.[9]

10. — § I – The text of the Provincial Directory is to be agreed by the Provincial Council of the Laity. It is sent to the Prior Provincial, who transmits it, together with his opinion and that of

---

6 Proposal by the International Congress of Lay Fraternities of St Dominic, Fatima, 2018.

7 DG2007, I § 4

8 DG1987, 1.

9 DG1987, 2.

INTERNATIONAL COUNCIL OF LAY DOMINICAN FRATERNITIES

his Council, to the Master of the Order for approval.

§ II – In approving the Provincial Directory, the Master of the Order may also make amendments to particular norms.

§ III – The approved Provincial Directory is promulgated by the Prior Provincial.[10]

11. — Unless provision is made by the National Directory, the Provincial Directory must determine:

1° the conditions for admission to a Fraternity;

2° the time of probation and of profession of the promise, without prejudice to no. 6 above;

3° the frequency of the Sacraments, and the prayers which the brothers and sisters of the Lay Fraternities are to raise to God;

4° the frequency of the meetings of the Fraternities and the form of their celebration, and also the frequency of spiritual conferences;

5° the internal constitution of each Fraternity and of the Fraternities of the Province as a whole;

6° the manner of proceeding for the election of officials, without prejudice to norms of the Rule and these Declarations;

7° the manner and limits of dispensation, without prejudice to no. 13 below;

8° suffrages for deceased brothers and sisters of the Lay Fraternities, and for the whole Order.[11]

12. — § I – Where several Provinces are present in the territory of a single nation, there may also be a National Directory. The National Directory provides norms for national structures of the Laity of St Dominic. It may also provide norms for Provinces and Fraternities, although a Provincial Directory may derogate from norms of the National Directory.

§ II – The text of the National Directory is to be agreed by the Provincial Councils of the Laity of the provinces concerned. It is to

---

10 DG1987, 1; DG2007, II § 1.
11 DG1987, 6.

32

be transmitted to the Master of the Order for approval together with the opinions of the Priors Provincial concerned and their Councils.

§ III – In approving the National Directory, the Master of the Order may also make amendments to particular norms.

§ IV – The approved National Directory is promulgated by the President of the national committee of Priors Provincial, if there is one, or else by the Master of the Order.[12]

13. — § I – The superiors of the Order and the presidents of the Fraternities do not have the authority to dispense from divine law or the universal law of the Church.

§ II – A dispensation always requires a just and reasonable cause (cf. can. 90 § 1). Norms which define essentially constitutive elements of an institute or act are not subject to dispensation (cf. can. 86).

§ III – Only the Master of the Order may dispense all Lay Dominicans from a norm of the Rule.

§ IV – The Prior Provincial may dispense individual fraternities from a norm of the Rule or the Directory, even without limit of time.

§ V – The President of the Fraternity may legitimately dispense from a norm of the Rule or the Directory in individual cases and for a determined time.[13]

14. — The Prior Provincial has the power to sanate invalid acts of the Fraternity, especially concerning admission to profession of the promise.[14]

Government of the Fraternity

15. — § I – Unless the Directory determines otherwise, the President and Council of the Fraternity are elected by the members of that Fraternity who have made at least the temporary promise.

§ II – To be elected President, a member must have made the

---

12 DG1987, 1; DG2007, II § 1.
13 DG2007, III.
14 DG1987, 4.

perpetual promise.

16. — § I – In accordance with art. 21(c) of the Rule, the Religious Assistant is to be a religious ("brother or sister") of the Order. If it is impossible to appoint a suitable Dominican religious as Assistant to a fraternity, the Prior Provincial may dispense from this requirement and appoint another suitably-qualified person to assist the members in doctrinal matters and the spiritual life in the Dominican tradition.[15]

§ II – A religious or cleric who is not under the jurisdiction of the Prior Provincial cannot validly be appointed Assistant without the written consent of his or her major superior. For a secular cleric this consent is given by his Ordinary.[16]

Government of the Fraternities in the Province

17. — § I – The Directory determines the manner of electing the Provincial President and the Provincial Council of the Laity.

§ II – To be elected Provincial President, a member must have made the perpetual promise.

18. — § I – In accordance with art. 20(b) of the Rule, the Provincial Promoter is to be a religious ("brother or sister") of the Order. Dispensation from this requirement is reserved to the Master of the Order.

§ II – One who is not under the jurisdiction of the Prior Provincial cannot validly be appointed Provincial Promoter without the written consent of his or her major superior and a signed agreement between the Prior Provincial and the Promoter.[17]

§ III – The term of office of the Provincial Promoter is four years. He or she may not serve for more than two consecutive terms.

§ IV – Although the Provincial Promoter has the full right to participate in meetings of the Lay Provincial Council, he or she does

---

15 DG2007, V.
16 ACG Trogir (2013), 187; Bologna (2016), 345.
17 DG2007, IV § 2.

not enjoy active or passive voice in any organ of the Lay Fraternities.[18]

Elections

19. — § I – Except where these Declarations or the Directory make other provision, elections among the Laity of St Dominic take place in accordance with cann. 119, 1° and 164–183.

§ II – Unless the Directory determines otherwise, there may be up to three scrutinies in an election. An absolute majority is required for election in the first or second scrutiny. If there have been two inconclusive scrutinies, a vote is to be taken between the two candidates with the greatest number of votes or, if there are more than two, between the two senior by first promise in the Lay Fraternities. After a third inconclusive scrutiny, that person is deemed elected who is senior by first promise in the Lay Fraternities.

Separation from the Lay Fraternities

20. — § I – At the expiry of the temporary promise, if it is not renewed, a member is free to depart from the Lay Fraternities.

§ II – During the time of the temporary promise, or after making the perpetual promise, a member is not to seek an indult to depart from the Lay Fraternities except for a grave reason weighed before God and with the assistance of fellow members. In the presence of such a reason, a motivated request is to be presented to the President of the Fraternity, who is to forward it to the Prior Provincial together with his/her own opinion and that of the Council of the Fraternity.

§ III – The Prior Provincial is competent to grant an indult of departure from the Lay Fraternities. Once the indult is notified in writing to the member concerned, he or she is dispensed from the promise and the requirement to observe the particular law of the Lay

---

18 DG2007, IV § 3.

Fraternities of St Dominic.[19]

21. — § I – Besides the situations mentioned in canon 316 § 1, a member who has made the temporary or perpetual promise may be dismissed for one of the following offences:

1° grave violation of the Rule or of the Directory;

2° causing grave public scandal among the faithful.

§ II – In the cases mentioned in § I, the President of the Fraternity is first to warn the member formally in writing.

§ III – If the warning is not heeded, the President with the consent of the Council of the Fraternity may ask the Prior Provincial to dismiss the member. In the situations mentioned in can. 316 § 1 the President must ask the Prior Provincial to dismiss the member.

§ IV – If the Prior Provincial, having afforded the member the opportunity to present a defence, judges the dismissal to be warranted, he issues a written decree of dismissal.

§ V – The decree of dismissal, once legitimately notified in writing to the member, brings about the cessation of rights and obligation deriving from the promise, and extends to all Lay Fraternities of St Dominic.

§ VI – Hierarchical recourse to the Master of the Order against a decree of dismissal is always possible.[20]

22. — § I – A member who has obtained an indult of departure from the Lay Fraternities and who subsequently seeks to be reincorporated in any Fraternity must follow the formation process again. The member's perpetual promise can be received only with the permission of the Prior Provincial with the consent of the Council of the member's new Fraternity. The promise and admission of one who keeps silent about a previous indult of departure is invalid.[21]

§ II – One who has been dismissed from the Lay Fraternities,

---

19 DG2007, VI § 1.
20 DG2007, VII §§ 1 and 3; can. 316 § 1.
21 DG2007, VI § 2.

after careful evaluation of his or her condition of life and with certainty of amendment, may be re-admitted under the same conditions as in § I.[22]

---

22 DG2007, VII § 2.

APPROVED
PROPOSALS

Approved Proposals

INTRODUCTION

Dear brothers and sisters

The moment has come to send you the Acts of the Congress and also the text of the new corpus of the Declarations of the Master of the Order. I must therefore call a number of important ideas to your attention as you receive these texts:

- The current declarations rescind all previous declarations. In fact, we have a new complete corpus of Declarations of the Master of the Order.
- The Provincial directories must be revised in accordance with the text of the Acts and of these declarations. In future publications of the directories, only these declarations must appear.
- Some of the proposals of the Congress have been changed. I was obliged to listen to the advice of the Procurator of the Order to ensure that they were in accord with the Rule and with canon law.
- One proposal made at the assembly does not remain in the

text because after due reflection, it was not possible to apply it.

- The declarations have force of law from the date on which they appear in the text itself.

I should like to thank once again those people who worked to allow us to have this text before Christmas: the Master of the Order for all his attention and for the letter that accompanies these Acts; the Procurator of the Order for his juridical aid; Isaura from Brazil who worked on the translation of the texts; Ruth Anne who also worked on the translations; and Edoardo for his help in formatting and preparing the final text.

Fr. Rui Carlos Antunes e Almeida Lopes OP

Rome, December 22, 2018

COMMISSION GOVERNMENT RULE AND STATUTES

Proposal 1

That fraternities/chapters be open to the accompaniment of the divorced and remarried, who desire full communion with the Church. Chapters may discern to guide them on their journey to "an awareness of their situation before God"(AL).

An individual seeking membership in a fraternity must demonstrate "humility, discretion and love for the Church and her teachings" (AL).

For this discernment to happen, fraternities are to conform with the Magisterium of the Church. If the local ordinary has expressly and in writing admitted a named individual back to the sacraments, the "special situation" need no longer be considered an impediment to reception and profession as a lay Dominican.

Proposal 2

According to the tradition of the Order and the spiritual meaning of the word Profession, which expresses better the nature of the link of the laity to the order of St Dominic, we recommend that the Order use the word Profession when relating to the Lay

Fraternities of Saint Dominic.

Proposal 3

With respect to different traditions there should be no confusion in the clothing worn by Lay Dominicans and a religious habit

Proposal 4

We recommend that rules 20c and 21b be amended to allow that Fraternity members and Provincial delegates or eligible voters can directly elect their respective presidents.

Proposal 5

In order to assist the ICLDF fulfil its mission statement we recommend that each Provincial Council/Vicariate annually submits before 31 May to the ICLDF and the Regional Council a report containing the following information; Name and location of fraternities, number of members and the stage in their profession within the fraternity, activities for the year, contact person with email address and telephone number. Statistical data aggregated from these reports will be published on the Lay Fraternities website.

Proposal 6

That, for future Congresses, clearer guidelines be provided to commissions that will empower them to develop discrete and concise proposals.

Proposal 7

We recommend that the provincial council promote an increased awareness of the importance of the work done by the ICLDF and the Regional Councils with the aim of improving communication with, and support of these councils and thus helping all Fraternities to work together as one body. The knowledge of these structures must be included as part of formation

Proposal 8

We recommend that it is the responsibility of each Provincial or Vicariate council to report to the Regional Council their contact person.

Proposal 9

Propose to amend Section I (B) (5) of the Statutes of the ICLDF to read as follows:

"5) -The Council shall elect from among its members a Coordinator. The Coordinator will be elected by the affirmative vote of a majority of its members present at a meeting where a quorum is present, and shall serve for a non-renewable period of three (3) years. The Coordinator shall also represent the Dominican Laity in the Board of the Dominican Family. If the Coordinator cannot be present at a Council meeting, he/she shall appoint another Council member to represent him/her, who shall have the Coordinator's proxy voting authority".

Proposal 10

In the event that the Coordinator's term as Regional representative expires before his/her term as ICLDF Coordinator, he/she shall continue to serve as ICLDF Coordinator for the remainder of his/her term. He shall no longer represent his/her Region and the newly appointed Regional representative shall then represent the particular Region".

Proposal 11

We recommend that Provincial/Vicarial Directories allow the Fraternities to grant partial dispensation from the initial formation during the period preceding the temporary profession, to those aspiring members coming from the International Dominican Youth

Movement (IDYM) who can verifiably demonstrate to have received equivalent Dominican Formation

COMMISSION FORMATION

This commission worked on the subject concerning Study and Training, developing three fundamental points:
1) Training
2) Dimensions of the training
3) Lay Former

Now, considering the resolutions emanated from the International Congress of Argentina in 2007 and the Rule of the Lay Fraternities of St Dominic in number 13, we made five proposals:

13. The main sources of Dominican formation are: - The Word of God and theological reflection. - The liturgical prayer. - The history and tradition of the Order. - The contemporary documents of the Church and the Order. - The study of the signs of the times

Proposal 1

The ICLDF must publish the Study and Formation program in 2019, considering the resolutions of the Pilar International Congress held in 2007 and those of the 2018 International Fatima Congress.

Each province, region or country will adapt it to its own realities

Proposal 2

FORMATION LEVELS:

1. Admission (initial formation)
2. Temporary profession
3. Perpetual profession (perpetual formation): with it the definitive incorporation into the secular branch of the Order is made.

The different Directories must determine, among other things:

a) The requirements for admission to the Fraternity.

b) The times of admission and profession or promise

Proposal 3

A) HUMAN FORMATION

Each fraternity is a small community of faith where human formation takes place, manifested through:

Growth in self-knowledge, discovering talents and limitations, learning to dialogue by listening and responding to others. Working together respecting diversity, exercising evangelical compassion, and experiencing and spreading Christian joy.

B) SPIRITUAL FORMATION

It consists in caring for the personal and communal prayer of the Word of God that challenges us to study it, contemplate it and preach it (Cf. Rule No. 10.)

C) THEOLOGICAL FORMATION

To give reason for their hope as Christians, the Dominican laity must have basically: solid theological formation, knowledge of the human sciences, documents of the Church, and of the Dominican tradition.

The study of a fundamental or spiritual theology course is recommended

D) APOSTOLIC FORMATION

The preaching is exercised in the daily encounter with the person, within the fraternity and in the fields of life and action, listening, sharing, and practicing compassion and mercy. Mainly promoting Justice and Peace and Care for Creation and "the unity of Christians and dialogue with non-believers". (Rule No. 12)

Proposal 4

FORMATOR PROFILE

1. It must be a lay brother or sister
2. Of perpetual profession
3. To be elected by the council for 3 years and may be re-elected
4. Possess good doctrinal preparation and knowledge of the Order
5. Demonstrate prudence in human relationships
6. Ability to value the person
7. Sensitivity to the problems of the candidate
8. Humility and capacity for listening and empathy

The head of formation of the local fraternity can be a member of the council or not, in which case it should be heard in relation to the formation and admission of candidates.

Proposal 5

INSTITUTE THE FIGURE OF THE PROVINCIAL FORMER WHO MUST BE CHOSEN BY THE RESPECTIVE COUNCIL. This prepares the formation program together with the provincial council and makes it known and coordinates with the formators of the fraternities that make up the province; who will develop it according to their province, country or region..

COMMISSION: FINANCE AND COMMUNICATION

COMMUNICATION

Proposal 1

We recommend that all regional and provincial councils appoint someone in charge of communications.

Proposal 2

We propose electronic mail as the preferred form of communication. alternative digital platforms can be used to communicate with our brothers and sisters and with the curia.

Proposal 3

We recommend: that all provincial council officers use electronic mail to communicate with the regional ICLDF representative and with the promoter general of the laity.

Proposal 4

We recommend that all changes to the provincial council officers be promptly communicated to the regional council, the regional ICLDF representative, and to the promoter general of the laity

Proposal 5

We encourage all provinces to send information such as the life of the fraternity to

webmaster@fraternitiesop.com

and to the general promoter for communication to

press@curia.op.org

Proposal 6

we recommend that key activities of the fraternities are to be communicated and reviewed regionally and shared internationally.

FINANCE

Proposal 1

The annual contribution to the ICDLF is to cover the cost of the annual international council meeting, other meetings, if needed, and to keep the cost of the international congress as low as possible.

Proposal 2

The ICLDF treasurer will produce an annual report of finances for the preceding year by february 15 of the current year. this report will be sent by the icldf webmaster to the provincial presidents and treasurers, whose emails should be provided..

Proposal 3

since we are a non profit organisation, surplus funds may be utilized to support dominican family projects in need of funds

Proposal 4

We recommend to keep the annual contribution to the

ICLDF at 1.50 euro per member per year, due not later than june 30.

COMMISSION: DOMINICAN FAMILY

NUNS

- Urge the Fraternities to have frequent encounters with the monasteries;
- Organize activities, share moments of formation, study and prayer.
- Require their intercession for particular needs of the Order, country and / or the world;
- Contribute to their needs.

FRIARS

- Discuss frequently, communicate news, request respect for lay autonomy.
- Require accompaniment to the Fraternities and inclusion in pastoral and missionary programs.

RELIGIOUS

- Engage in a fraternal dialogue with the religious and lay people involved in their works.

- Open to mutual participation in spaces of formation, prayer, community and mission.

LAITY

- Respect differences with institutions, movements, groups and promote mutual inclusion.
- To build bridges to form a community, to urge spaces of common mission.
- Encourage the laity to be, as Pope Francis asks, the Church on the way out, preventing them from nesting in convent houses and / or sacristy.

YOUTH

- Recognize their identity, their own characteristics, but also common objectives.
- Integrate them with full rights to the OP Family and its mission.

GENERAL PROPOSALS.

- Organize vocational networks with participation of all branches.
- Propose common missions of preaching, where community life and the experience of the pillars of the Order are facilitated.
- Participate in councils and/or Secretariats of Family OP, propose their creation where they do not exist.

RELATIONSHIP WITH THE CHURCH

- Become aware of the eminently ecclesial character of the Order.
- Actively join the parishes, lay organizations and spaces of the local Church

COMMISSION: PREACHING AND PRAYER

1. [*Declaration*] Lay Preaching aims at introducing Jesus and sharing the Gospels into our world, in the context of family, friends, neighbors, people at work, in the social media and other contexts.

   Lay Preachers should be able to listen, to try to understand and to truly love those they preach to.

   Lay Preaching is not only about teaching, but about listening and learning and being present.

   Clerical Preaching and Lay Preaching do not exclude one another.

2. [*Declaration*] The compassion of Jesus for all humanity and our compassion urge us to preach.

   Lay Preaching can take on many forms depending on the gifts given to us by God, for example singing and making music and other contributions to an attractive liturgy, art, writing, publishing and film making, listening and spiritual guidance, works of charity, advocacy for the marginalized, the ability to serve, and more.

We should be able to talk about the gospel, our personal faith and the teachings of the church.

The way we live our lives is also a way of preaching. How we live our lives should make other people curious about our faith. Preaching requires that we learn to listen, to understand the signs of our times and to react to them

3.   [*Commendation*] We should be praying for occasions to preach

4.   [*Commendation*] Social media and other forms of modern technology need to be used in order to reach out to people in the modern world.

5.   [*Commendation*] During formation, members should be encouraged and supported by their fraternity to investigate and develop their individual form of preaching according to their gifts.

6.   [Declaration] We belong to lay fraternities in the Order of Preachers because God called us to them. Our fraternities should be places of healing, compassion and joy and also places of prayer. Our fraternities should be places of ongoing formation on our way to being preachers. They should be places in which we share our experiences and in which we receive support.

The life in our fraternities should reflect Jesus' words in John 17,11: "that they may be one, even as we are one", thus making our fraternities into a way of preaching

7.   [*Commendation*] We recommend that each fraternity should look for common preaching projects. Making use of the individual charisms of its members, such projects help the fraternity in its development as a fraternity. Community projects encourage new

ideas, release energy, creating new life and new commitment within the fraternity. (Compare Acts of General Chapter in Bologna 2016, article 126)

8. [[*Declaration*] Number 10 of the Lay Dominican Rule offers us a list of spiritual sources which help to nourish and support our contemplative and apostolic vocation.

9. [*Commendation*] We propose that the fraternities meet from time to time to reflect upon and discuss with one another their spiritual growth with the intention of renewing their commitment. This may require help from outside.

10. [*Commendation*] In the present situation of great upheaval in the Church (problem of child abuse by priests, discussion about marriage and divorce and about homosexuality) we recommend that Lay Dominicans should deepen their understanding of and renew their relationship to the Sacraments of the Eucharist and Reconciliation.

11. [Declaration] As Lay Dominicans our personal prayer and the sources mentioned in Number 10 of the Rule should enlighten our work, family life and social activities.
    Through our fraternities we are connected to God and the Church. This connection should be of primary importance to all members.
    Being in the world, but not of the world (see Joh 17,14), we are called to sanctify the world with the help of God.

12. [/*Commendation*] We encourage the fraternities to help their members to develop their personal prayer.

COMMISSION: JUSTICE PEACE AND CARE OF CREATION

BACKGROUND:

As Church teachings and all the general chapters of the Order in the last 50 years have affirmed, work for Justice and Peace is a constitutive dimension of evangelization.

As counselled by the Master of the Order at this Congress, **we propose**

RESOLUTION:

That lay fraternities everywhere reflect on where injustices are present in our own personal and communal relationships and structures and address them, so that we can be credible preachers of Justice and Peace.

BACKGROUND:

Given that justice and peace is an integral part of our vocation as lay Dominicans;

inspired by the two witness statements from Venezuela and Cameroon;

and since the International Dominican Commission for Justice and Peace consists of all 5 branches of the Dominican

Family,

we propose

RESOLUTION:

That each local community (chapter, fraternity, group etc) shall have a clearly defined contact person responsible for communication and activity on issues of Justice and Peace.

BACKGROUND:

Given that friars and sisters have structures for Justice and Peace at every level, and

That it is necessary to have a means of communication related to Justice and Peace between local, national and international levels of the Dominican laity and with the Dominican Family

We propose

RESOLUTION:

That every level of Dominican Laity in addition to the local fraternity (e.g. provincial/national, regional, international) include an identifiable Justice, Peace and Care of Creation contact person responsible for interaction among the levels and with the Dominican Family.

RESOLUTION:

That a database of the contact people for Justice and Peace in the chapters/fraternities be established and maintained by the Lay Provincial Council.

RESOLUTION:

That the Lay Dominicans on the International Dominican Commission for Justice and Peace (IDCJP) send information and alerts through the International Council of Lay Dominican Fraternities (ICLDF) to enable local fraternities to consider ways to show solidarity with Dominicans in difficult situations.

RESOLUTION:

That all lay fraternities be made aware that our Order has a presence at the United Nations centers in Geneva, New York, Vienna and Nairobi to facilitate evangelization at the global level. Our UN delegations engage with governments to support the actions of Dominicans for justice and human rights at the ground level.

RESOLUTION:

That Lay Dominican formation integrate Justice, Peace and Care of Creation through all aspects of holistic Gospel-based formation (Human, Spiritual, Intellectual and Pastoral/Apostolic) and all stages of formation from initial to ongoing.

RESOLUTION:

That intellectual formation includes Catholic Social Teachings and Dominican resources on Justice and Peace.

RESOLUTION:

Equipping Lay Dominicans with skills to engage in conflict resolution, peace-building and combatting injustices should be undertaken in close collaboration, whenever possible, with Justice and Peace coordinators in other branches of the Dominican Family and other relevant organizations.

BACKGROUND:

In 2017, the Master of the Order initiated an annual Dominican month for peace from the first Sunday of Advent until the Church's World Day of Peace on January 1. The focus in 2018 will be on the Democratic Republic of Congo.

We propose

RESOLUTION:

That all Lay Dominican chapters / fraternities include activities for the Dominican Month for Peace in their annual planning.

COMMISSION: PROMOTERS AND ASSISTANT

I. THE PROFILE OF PROMOTERS AND RELIGIOUS ASSISTANTS

A. PROVINCIAL PROMOTER
The Provincial Promoter is a Dominican friar under full jurisdiction of his Prior Provincial who serves as a liaison between Lay Dominicans and the Prior Provincial. He is appointed to a four (4) year term by the Prior). He is a non-voting member of the Lay Provincial Council and other councils as identified by the Lay Provincial President. The Provincial Promoter collaborates with the Promoter General of the Laity to support the mission and vision of the Lay Dominican fraternities specifically in the areas of Justice, Peace and Care of Creation.

B. RELIGIOUS ASSISTANT
The Religious Assistant is one of the following: a Dominican friar, Dominican nun, Dominican cooperator brother, Lay Dominican permanent deacon, perpetually professed lay Dominican

(male or female), a sister of the Dominican Family, a secular priest, or a religious of another Order/Congregation that assists an individual fraternity in spiritual and theological matters. If a Religious Assistant is not a member of the Order of Preachers, s/he must obtain authorization from her/his superior and ensure that s/he is duly prepared on Dominican history and spirituality. The Religious Assistant is a non-voting member of the fraternity and is appointed for a three or four year term by the Prior Provincial.

C.   COMMON TO BOTH

The Provincial Promoter and Religious Assistant follow the example of 2 Corinthians 1:24: "It is not that we are trying to rule over your faith, but rather to work with you for your joy".

II.   CLARIFICATIONS OF THEIR FUNCTIONS

A.   PROVINCIAL PROMOTER

1.   The Provincial Promoter should possess an affability, an interest in, and an enthusiasm for in the Lay Dominicans and be capable of listening to and interacting with members of the Laity on all social and academic levels, fostering participation of Lay members in the preaching work of the Church as well as in established ministries of the Province.

2.   The Provincial Promoter should be available to render advice and provide support to the Lay Provincial President and Lay Provincial Councils. The Promoter visits fraternities with the Lay Provincial President and/or designee from among the Lay Provincial officers as scheduled. He works in concert with the Lay Provincial Council to identify and evaluate fraternities'

and members' needs and/or interventions to strengthen community life and the individual Lay vocation. The Provincial Promoter further collaborates with the Lay Provincial President in developing reports on the Laity for submission to the Prior Provincial and his Council.

3. The Provincial Promoter reviews and processes to the Prior Provincial those recommendations submitted by the Lay Provincial President or Council relating to status changes of members or fraternities. He promptly notifies the Lay Provincial Council in writing of the determination made by the Prior Provincial that includes justification of the decision. This includes, but is not limited to, the appointment or removal of a Religious Assistant, the petitions to extend a term of office in service, the erection or suppression of a fraternity, etc.

4. The Provincial Promoter openly communicates with the Province by informing the Lay Council of matters or concerns issued from the friars' General and Provincial Chapters, the Order and Province, and those specific matters related to the Laity. He facilitates communication between the Lay Dominicans, friars and religious to enhance the mission of the Laity and Order in general. The Provincial Promoter also ensures that Lay Dominicans are invited to events (e.g. meetings, talks, special celebrations, etc.) taking place on a Provincial level.

5. The Provincial Promoter encourages and identifies friars and religious to serve Lay Dominican fraternities as Religious Assistants and/or to provide theological, spiritual, and pastoral lectures/ workshops for the fraternities.

6. The Provincial Promoter fosters initiatives by Lay

Dominicans on Justice, Peace and Care of Creation.

7. The Provincial Promoter provides insight on Dominican spirituality, history, theology, and Church teachings appropriate to lay vocations. He contributes written articles for a Lay Province's newsletter or Dominican provincial periodical on a regular basis.

B. RELIGIOUS ASSISTANT

1. The Religious Assistant attends fraternity and council meetings when possible to encourage and promote the evangelical and apostolic works of the members and the Fraternity.

2. The Religious Assistant recommends study topics and provides spiritual and theological commentary to aid a fraternity's formation and study as needed, providing advice to those members who are presenting the materials.

3. The Religious Assistant assists the fraternity's Council in the discernment process of a member's advancement in the Order and assists the fraternity's President with the Rites of Reception and Profession.

4. The Religious Assistant may recommend lay speakers or priests (as required) for days of recollection, retreats, spiritual direction, etc.

5. The Religious Assistant prays for an increase of Lay Dominican vocations and for the members' spiritual growth, mission, apostolic activities, and attentiveness to the goals of the Church.

6. The Religious Assistant communicates with the Provincial Promoter on a regular basis.

ACTS
OF THE CONGRESS

Acts of the Congress

**FRATRES ORDINIS PRÆDICATORUM
CURIA GENERALITIA**

Rome December 12, 2018

To the laity of the Order of Preachers

Prot.73/17/810 ICLDF

Dear sisters and brothers,

It is with joy, that I write these lines to accompany the publication of the Acts of the International Assembly of Dominican Lay Fraternities that was held in Fatima last October. Even if we cannot assimilate them with the Acts of what could be a «general chapter of lay Dominicans» that would formulate decisions, they reflect the richness of the reflection that was conducted by your representatives and formulate guidelines that in my opinion are very important for the coming years. I therefore invite you all not only to read them, but also to study them in fraternities and regions, so that, according to the specificities of each province, these orientations contribute to strengthening, ever more, communion among all.

Such an assembly is certainly the moment when everyone can become aware of both the place of the concern for communion in our common purpose of evangelization following Saint Dominic and the diversity of cultures, socio-political and ecclesial situations of one another. For this reason, this type of assembly, like the provincial chapters of the laity, always invites us to put into practice this patient democratic research of the unanimity that characterizes the tradition of our Order. The challenge of dialogue at the heart of this diversity, which is a true richness of the Order, is precisely to make sure that the orientations which we take together do not hold their value first because they represent a majority opinion but because they have been discerned by all as steps to be taken together. Thus our diversities may humbly recognize that they all have to draw from the same first source of communion. At a moment in time when the universal Church emphasizes synodality, the Order of Preachers, in its different branches and in the synergy between them, offers a style of synodality which is all the more relevant because it is tuned to evangelization and to the proclamation of the approach of the Kingdom. It seems to me that the assembly of Fatima was marked by this conviction.

The orientations that have been formulated constitute a sort of roadmap for all of us, and especially for the International Council of Fraternities and the General Promoter of the Dominican Laity. I invite them, as well as those in charge of the laity of the Order on provincial level and the councils, to establish their programme of animation, promotion and accompaniment from the study of these orientations. Here we have a beautiful and demanding programme aimed at stimulating the Dominican lay vocation and at carrying out the service which this vocation wishes to bring to the Church and to the local Churches. I am convinced our time opens a page of the history of the Church where the essential role of the laity in the mission of evangelization of the Church will increasingly be recognized, valued and called on. With its available means, the Order would like to contribute to this renewal of evangelization through the commitment of its laity and through the synergy between all the branches of an Order which is know to proclaim the friendship of God through the double evangelical and apostolic witness of its fraternities and communities.

The assembly of Fatima did not fail to highlight the apostolic horizon of the Order. The theme which was the thread of these days of meeting, Justice, Peace and Care of Creation, made it possible to know more about the richness of the current commitments of each other. It also led to the identification of certain challenges to be met, of mobilizations to be reinforced, of solidarities to be deployed, of theological themes to be deepened, of misunderstandings to be lifted. Above all, the study of these questions has led to emphasize how much this field was a privileged theological place to make the teachings and the wisdom of the Church in matter of social doctrine better known, while at the same time explaining their theological foundations. This is beyond doubt a privileged path for evangelization. In doing so, the assembly did not neglect to address the other dimensions of the participation of the laity in the proclamation of the Gospel, either through proposals specific to the Order, or through participation in the life and mission of the local churches. This theme of the proclamation of the Gospel once again proved the most accurate horizon for speaking of the Dominican family, of the vocation of the Order as a whole, and of reciprocity in the apostolic responsibility which must be the leaven of unity, development and joy.

As you read these Acts, you will find that the theme of the initial and permanent formation, particularly caught the attention of the assembly. I am particularly pleased with this because it seems to me that through this priority given to formation and study, it is a question of really giving top priority to the promotion of each one's proper Dominican vocation. Formation should not be reduced to the sole dimension of study but should as much as possible be all encompassing, as a way of saying today what was Dominic's concern: may his brothers not «do» the preaching but let them «be» preachers. May their desire to live for the proclamation of the Gospel guide their whole life, individual and community, may they learn to live from the mystery they proclaim and truly become what they are called to become. In the end, could one better say what the Church is?

In the service of this Dominican lay vocation, the Order has put in place a Rule, various structures and modes of accompaniment. The assembly studied a certain number of issues in these areas, for example by asking for the establishment of a manner of communication that best serves the unity and synergy of all, clarifying the content of the function of religious assistant, proposing some amendments to the Rule. It is in this sense that, in accordance with what is expected of the Master of the Order, I will promulgate a new more synthetic version of the ordinations of the Rule. I will present the few amendments envisaged in the Rule to the Holy See for approval, so that it is closer to the reality of the life of the fraternities.

Two more points to conclude. The first is the importance that the Order must continue to give to the development of «International Dominican Youth Movement » Of course, for some young people of this movement, their commitment will be a great preparation to join the Fraternities when time comes. But, above all, this Dominican youth movement must be considered by all of us as the way in which the Order, drawing on its long tradition, wishes to contribute to calling young people and to accompanying those who, during the years of their youth, wish to live the mystery of their baptism by proclaiming the Gospel. The second is the attention that the assembly has given to the reception of people who live in difficult personal, family, marital situations and, sometimes, far from the discipline of the Church. It does not take them away from faith, nor does it separate them from the fraternity of the Church, It is the duty of the Order, which is the Order of Mercy, to bear witness to this.

The vitality of the Dominican laity is a grace for the whole Order and for the radiance of its vocation to proclaim the approach of the Kingdom. I would like to conclude this letter in expressing my deepest and most sincere gratitude. This vitality must call on the whole Order to continually immerse further into the world, in order to immerse ever deeper into the mystery of this God-with-us whom we will be celebrating very soon. With all of you, I entrust this vocation to Our Lady, Mary, Mother of Preachers.

Your brother in Saint Dominic

fr Bruno Cadore, o.p.
Master of the Order of Preachers

List of Participants

Josefa Librace; Argentina

Salvador Librace; Argentina

Silvia Beatriz Molina De Guillen; Argentina

María Teresa Tenti; Argentina

Robert Bautista; Australia

Stephen Peterson; Australia

Ludovic Namurois; Belgique

Maria De Lourdes Lear Dos Santos; Brasil

Bogdan Penev; Bulgaria

Fr. Aristide Basse; Cameroun

Cecile Pierre Elise Chatap; Cameroun

Kouossu Clementine; Cameroun

Felix Foko; Cameroun

Elise Constance Lessako Noah; Cameroun

Bridget Ngam; Cameroun

Charlotte Ngougni Epse Fovop; Cameroun

Margaret Nubia Fofung Epse Fogam; Cameroun

Joseph Sama (Dr); Cameroun

Severine Tchoula Tameko; Cameroun

Emma Visas Ngwe; Cameroun

Gisele Blanette Yaka Nyamsi; Cameroun

Benoît Des Roches; Canada

Catherine Halstead; Canada

Konrad Hanz; Canada

Paulina Rosa Arroyo Henriquez; Chile

Teresa De La Mercedes Pino Mendez; Chile

Diva Amparo Moreno Triviño; Colombia

Sehinabou Yolande Doukoure; Cote D'ivoire

Aya Alphonsine Kouassi-M'bengue; Cote D'ivoire

Guillermo García Bregado; Cuba

Fr. Rui Carlos Antunes e Almeida Lopes; Curia

Fr. Vivian Boland; Curia

Fr. Bruno Cadré; Curia

Fr. Michael Deeb; Curia

Fr. Miguel Angel Del Rio; Curia

Sr. Cecilia Espenilla; Curia

Sr. Marie-Teho Manaud; Curia

Fr. Krzysztof Poplawski; Curia

Fr. Luis Javier Rubio; Curia

Fr. Orlando Rueda Acevedo; Curia

Fr. Gerard Francisco Timoner Iii; Curia

Fr. Charles Emeka Ukwe;Curia

Sr. Letizia Youchtchenko; Curia

Ivan Bok; Czech Republic

Eva Fuchsova; Czech Republic

Fr. Hyacint Ullman; Czech Republic

Melba Marzia Hurdado De Rendon; Ecuador

Melba Del Carmen Rendon Hurtado; Ecuador

Luke Loquen; France

Klaus Bornewasser; Germany

Margarete Burkart; Germany

Melanie Delpech; Germany

Hans Gasper; Germany

Fr. David Michael Kammler; Germany

Volker Nebel; Germany

Leonor Aguilar Orellana; Guatemala

María Guadalupe Celis-Hecht Evans; Guatemala

Leonor Mercedes Chocano Aguilar; Guatemala

Fr. Ferenc Máté Barna; Hungary

Hilda Kőrösiné Merkl; Hungary

Joan Geraghty; Ireland

Patrick Hickey; Ireland

Paula Hickey; Ireland

Damien Mcdonnell; Ireland

Fr. Antonio Cocolicchio; Italy

Ruth Anne Henderson; Italy

Edoardo Mattei; Italy

Anisoara Tatar; Italy

Joseph Karanu; Kenya

Jean-Claude Loba Mkole; Kenya

Elisabeth Nyembo Aziza (Mrs Loba); Kenya

John Odhiambo Magambo; Kenya

Caren Onyango; Kenya

Catherine Sonye; Kenya

Inga Maria Ilarienė; Lithuania

Vilija Marija Semetiene; Lithuania

Lazaro Gomez; Mexico

Guillermo Rojas; México

Karin Bornhijm; Netherlands

Fr. Gerard Braks; Netherlands

Fr. Moses Arung; Nigeria

Callistus Carlton Okwudili Ileka; Nigeria

Nkechinyem Esther Nwaezeamaka; Nigeria

Anthony Obi; Nigeria

Fr. Joseph Osunde; Nigeria

Jan Frederik Solem; Norway

Elva (Susana) Brittos; Paraguay

Marina Duarte; Paraguay

Roque Jorgelina Maldonado; Paraguay

Elianny Martínez; Paraguay

Dario Rogelio Recalde Gamarra; Paraguay

Ilce Tongshi Quispe Rojas;

Peru

Carlos Teran; Peru

Gerardo Zamora Herrera; Peru

Fr. Giuseppe-Pietro Arsciwals; Philippines

Belen L. Tangco, Philippines

IDYM Benz Rodil; Philippines

Estrella Jona Tabayoyong; Philippines

Małgorzata Kopczyńska; Poland

Jacek Zejma; Poland

Cristina Busto; Portugal

Mariana Teresa Cardoso Ary Portocarrero De Almada De Sousa Cardoso; Portugal

António José. Carlos; Portugal

Maria Fernanda Carlos; Portugal

Sr. Celina Laranjeiro; Portugal

Maria De Lurdes Santos; Portugal

Gabriel Silva; Portugal

Sr. Conceição ; Portugal

Sr. Lissette Avilés-Ríos; Puerto Rico

Maria Cardenales Rodriguez; Puerto Rico

Hector Marquez; Puerto Rico

María Auxiliadora Come Rodriguez; Republica Dominicana

Beatriz Santaella; Republica Dominicana

Rihanna Dada Mukola Lutama;

Republique Democratique Du Congo

Genevieve Kantareme; Ruanda

Duncan Maclaren; Scottish

Eva Zudorova; Slovakia

Delores Rose Hartzenberg; South Africa

Frederick Philip Hartzenberg; South Africa

Khunjulwa Pearl Petrus; South Africa

Maposholi Tabile; South Africa

Fr. Juan Carlos Cordero; Spain

IDYM Monica Marco; Spain

Antonio-Jesus Rodriguez Hernandez; Spain

Jose Vicente Vila Castellar; Spain

Cynthia Donnelly; Usa

Denise Harvey; Usa

Michael Harvey; Usa

Cosette D Heimann Heimann; Usa

Marianne T Jablonski Jablonski; Usa

John Thomas Charles Keenan; Usa

Joseph Komadina; Usa

Jonathan Stabhl; Usa

Fr. Gerald Stookey; Usa

Joaquin Wong; Usa

Wiliy Rivero; Venezuela

Maria Hoang; Vietnam

Rosa Nguyen; Vietnam

COMMISSION AND CHAIRS

Government, Rules and Statutes

- Chair: Hector L. Marquez, OP
- Co-Chair: Rev. Fr. Honorato C. Castigador, OP

Communications & Finances

- Chair: Klaus Bornewasser, OP
- Co-Chair: Edoardo Mattei, OP
    - Member: Pedro Torres, OP

Study and Formation

- Chair: Eva Zudorova, OP
- Co-Chair: Catherine Masson, OP

Prayer & Preaching

- Chair: Felix Foko Fovo,OP
- Co-Chair: Gabriel Silva, OP
    - Member: Marcus Kejungki, OP

Justice and Peace and Care of Creation

- Chair: Joseph Komadina, OP
- Co-Chair: Catherine Neugebauer, OP
  - Supporting Co-Chairs: Duncan MacLaren, OP
  - Rev. Fr. Michael Deeb, O.P.

On Relations with the Church and the Dominican Family

- Chair: Teresita Tenti de Volta, OP
- Co-Chair: Susanna Brittos, OP

On Promoters

- Chair: Rev. Fr. Rui Carlos Lopes, OP

FRATRES ORDINIS PRÆDICATORUM
CURIA GENERALITIA

Rome, September 12, 2018

To fr Rui Carlos Antunes e Almeida Lopes, o.p.
General Promotor of Laity for the Order

To Hector L. Marquez, l.o.p., President

To all the participants of the International Assembly of Dominican Laity

Prot. 73/17/810/ICLDF

Dear fr Rui,
Dear fr Hector,
Dear Brothers and Sisters,

Now is the time for the meeting of the international assembly of the laity of the Order and, with this letter, I wish to join you all who are in Fatima for this meeting. I express the wish that these days, for all of you, might be days of deep joy, days of healing for the vocation of each and every one of us, days also for strengthening our conviction to be sent as preachers to the world with a common apostolic responsibility to serve the mission of Christ through all forms of evangelization.

I planned to participate in most of this assembly. Unfortunately,

I will not be able to do so because I was elected as one of the ten religious superiors who are members of the synod for young people. I will only be able to join you for one weekend, and I apologize for that, as I thank the organizers for agreeing to change the schedule so that we can better work together during these two days. It is indeed important for the Master of the Order to have this time to listen to the concerns of the laity of the Order, and to discern with them the directions that should be promoted and implemented for the good of preaching.

In the letter 1 sent to the laity of the Order at the beginning of this year, thinking of the assembly you are holding these days, l wrote that the latter would be the « celebration of the grace that is made to the Order, to have lay sisters and brothers as active members of its mission ». It is really the conviction that occupies me. It seems to me that it is a time of profound change for the Church itself, as well as for the way in which the Church is in the world. Evangelization is increasingly understood as being the proper work of the ecclesial communities, testifying by friendship and fraternity, to the will of Christ to « live familiarly with mankind, thus inspiring trust in all who go to him ». From this affirmation of Thomas Aquinas, which I like to quote because it seems to me to express the vocation of the Order of Preachers, I think we can retain some points of particular attention. The first is the reminder that the Order's vocation is to serve the mission of Christ. We always risk forgetting this by letting ourselves get locked into the sole consideration of our structures, our organizations, our own achievements and projects, our internal difficulties and sometimes our pride. But our vocation is above all to serve Christ's desire for familiarity with men and women.

The term familiarity emphasizes a second point of attention: there are steps to be taken to be really familiar with the world, there are displacements to effect, agreeing to let go of certain certainties.

Christian culture is no longer familiar to people in many places and often we lament it without noting well that it is up to us to open new paths to the truth with those we would like to join, to build new bridges, to find new forms of friendship.

And this leads us to a third point of attention: « May all have the confidence to go to him ». In evangelization, it is a question of an exchange of trust: trust of Christ, trust of people; confidence of the Church, confidence of the world!

The body of the preachers, in the diversity of their states of life, in the complementarity of their vocations, must be the place where we teach each other, awakening to these three attentions: to the primacy of the mission of Christ, to the requirement of putting the proposal of the familiar friendship of God at the heart of preaching, to trust in the name of God. My letter at the beginning of the year expressed the eminent role of the laity of the Order in calling us to this.

To call the entire Order to this. This is how, I believe, we must today discern the specific vocation of the laity within the vocation of the Order of Preachers to evangelization. The subjects I mentioned in my letter (the sign of fraternity, the gospel of the family, the worlds of youth, faith in dialogue, the accompaniment of life) indicate so many areas in which the laity of the Order are undoubtedly essential « protagonists » to respond to our common vocation for evangelization. It means both their creativity, as is asked of all other members of the Order, and dialogue between us, so that the specific experience of the laity, in the diversity of their human, social, professional, ecclesial and cultural rootedness, might be a stimulant of the common apostolic responsibility to which we are all called. We must seek the most appropriate means to make this happen, to strengthen fidelity to our vocation, so as to consolidate continually our service to the mission of the Church.

As I wrote in that letter, I therefore again wish that your assembly will be an essential part of this concern for the Order's own vocation to evangelization. Saying this, I do not want to encourage you to hold theoretical or idealistic discourses on what the evangelization of the Order should be. I would rather recall that it is this vocation, this determination to put our lives at stake on account of evangelization, which is the essential criterion of all that we can organize within our Order. It is the service of the mission of Christ that must guide the way to offer programmes of initial or permanent formation to the new laity who join us. It is the willingness of the witness of fraternity that can enlighten what we have to implement in terms of communication. It is solidarity in a single fraternity that provides benchmarks for the management of our finances in justice and equity. It is the contemplation of Christ the preacher that is the foundation of a spiritual life that can be the source of preaching. It is the very prayer of Christ sent by the Father that gives us confidence in our own ability to keep us in unity. This is to say how much the workshops that are planned during this assembly will have the task of proposing orientations for our« structures >> so that these offer the best conditions for the realization of the lay vocation within the Order and the Church.

The general assembly that you constitute will certainly be a wonderful experience of the Order's richness and diversity in the world. It will also be a great opportunity to experience the « sign of fraternity >> through which the Order of St Dominic wishes to be a servant of the communion that is at the heart of Jesus' prayer. At our meetings, one of the manifestations of this fraternity is the quality of our dialogues, as well as listening to each one with respect, trust and charity. Such an « ethics of the word exchanged » between brothers and sisters is demanding. But it is the pledge of our common conviction that through our diversity of opinions, of the interpretation of situations and what is at stake in them, of the identification of the priority challenges for evangelization, and of visions of the world, the fraternity that is given to us is the path to the common search for this truth that makes us free. May the Lord give us the grace of such an experience!

Once again, I apologize for not being able to be with you for the whole duration of your meeting. Nevertheless, I am looking forward to the two days during which I will be able to join you and, until that time, I assure you of my fraternal friendship, entrusting you to the intercession of Mary, Mother of Preachers, of Saint Dominic, and of all the saints of the Order.

Your brother in St Dominic,

fr Bruno Cadore, o.p.
Maestro dell'Ordine dei Predicatori

WELCOME WORDS

HÉCTOR L. MÁRQUEZ, O.P.
Coordinator of the International Council
of Dominican Lay Fraternities

Good morning, dear brothers and sisters in Saint Dominic!

Welcome to Fatima, Portugal, and to the Third International Congress of Lay Dominican Fraternities.

We have come here from all continents, answering the call to gather that the members of the International Council did, under the slogan: "Justice, Peace, and Care of Creation", sheltered under the protective mantle of Our Lady of the Rosary of Fatima and the inspiration and intercession of our Father Saint Dominic, who every day fulfill that promise he made to his brothers with his last breath, that after his death would help us more than he did in life.

With this protection and inspiration, during the next seven days we will meet in various committees, in addition to the plenary sessions, to discuss topics of common interest related to the different aspects of our fraternal life and how to improve our

Organization, reaffirm our identity and belonging to the Dominican Family in general, but particularly our membership of the Order of Preachers, as one of the three traditional branches of this meritorious Order founded by our Holy Father Dominic, and what this implies for the lives of each and every one of us and our fraternities.

On Sunday we will join our brother and General Master of the Order Bros.

Bruno Cadorè who, in according our rule, «as the successor of Santo Domingo and head of the Dominican Family presides all the fraternities of the world. »

Today we are accompanied by several members of the General Curia of the Order, namely, Bros. Miguel Ángel del Rio, Vicar of the Master, Bros. Orlando Rueda, Socius of the Master for Apostolic Life, Bros. Vivian Boland, Socius for Fraternal Life and Formation, Bros. Javier Abanto, General Promoter of Social Communication, Bros. Michael Deeb, General Promoter of Justice and Peace and Permanent Delegate for the United Nations, and, of course, our Bros. Rui Carlos Antunes e Almeida Lopes, Promoter General of the Laity who, as such, represents the General Master in all fraternities.

There are so many brothers and sisters who have helped us to make this Congress a reality that it would be impossible to name them all. However, I have to highlight the tireless work of the Secretary General of the Congress, our sister Belén Tangco of the Philippines, who started her work from the same day we decided on the place and date of the Congress at the meeting in June 2016, and still continues. To her our gratitude and the deserved applause of this Assembly.

Personally, to conclude my service to the Order and the Laity as Coordinator of the International Council of Lay fraternities Dominican, I thank God and the intercession of our Father Saint Dominic, the unexpected opportunity to know and share with so many brothers and sisters, laity, nuns, sisters of Apostolic Life, and friars from all over the world, who have enriched my life and contributed to reaffirming my Dominican vocation. Everyone, including you, will always carry you in my heart.

It is these international meetings that allow us to appreciate in all its grandeur the nature, scope and spiritual richness of our beloved Order, and to strengthen the bonds of brotherhood that unite us. I therefore urge you, when you return to your home countries, to share this experience with the brothers and sisters of your fraternities, regions, provinces and countries, and "fall in love", so that in our next international Congress multiply the number of participants.

Before concluding these brief words, I urge you to hug the brother or sister you have at your side and tell you: how good is to be Dominicans!

With these words I declare formally opened the work of this Congress, imploring the blessing of God, the Blessed Virgin Mary in her dedication to Our Lady of the Rosary, and our Father Santo Domingo.

Thank you for being here

Opening Address

FR RUI CARLOS ANTUNES E ALMEIDA LOPES, O.P.
Promotor General of Laity

Dear brothers and sisters

It is a great joy for me to welcome you all. So that we can have an idea of who is present at the assembly, I would like you to stand up when your region is called:

- Africa
- North America: United States and Canada.
- Latin America
- Asia Pacific
- Europe
- Curia.

I especially want to greet all those who live in regions with difficult situations, and if I may I want to welcome especially our brother who lives in Venezuela, a country torn by suffering and extreme poverty. There are difficult situations also in Cameroon, which is well represented here, and let us think of the Dominican Family in countries with very unstable situations such as the Central

African Republic and of course Iraq. I ask you all to remember them in your prayers.

As Promoter I want to thank especially the Master of the Order and the Curia for all their support of this initiative.

I want to thank the management of the Steyler Hotel in the person of the manager and my good friend P. Jose Augusto Leitão and Catarina Neves who has devoted so much attention to preparation of the Congress.

I thank the Province of Portugal and especially the Dominican Laity of Portugal for all the readiness to help and fraternal spirit they have shown. I thank the Nuns of the Pius XII Monastery and the Congregation of the Dominican Sisters of Saint Catherine of Siena (my sisters) for their support of this Congress.

There are people who are the soul of this Congress: certainly the International Council of the Laity with a special mention for the Secretary General of the Congress: Belen Tangco - for three months with about fifteen emails and messages per day we worked together; another for our dear Klaus who has done wonders with the restricted funds available. And again a word of thanks for two people: Edoardo Mattei, our webmaster: every week we had a meeting to evaluate the situation and we thank him for all his work on the website for registration and information. Not having a staff in Rome for all this, Edoardo has been invaluable throughout the preparation. And I thank Ruth Anne for her willingness and efficiency in all that was asked of her.

Inevitably, at an event like this there are shortcomings, for which I apologize, but I appeal to your sense of brotherhood: we are in our family here, so please cast a fraternal eye even on what is not perfect.

This is where I would like to begin my talk: the sense of fraternity. Over the last few years, I have had the opportunity to meet many lay Dominicans all over the world: what beautiful experiences I have had and shared! The Dominican Laity really does wonderful things and these really testify to their spirit as preachers.

There are, however, great challenges: recent history does not show openness to the Order as a whole. For the first time in history, at the time of the Congress on the Mission of the Order at the end of the Jubilee, the Laity appeared in the Dominican Family at this international level as a body: at that congress 60% of the participants were members of the Laity. And let's be clear: the religious had financial support that the Laity did not have: that says a lot.

But I must admit that the Laity has not yet reached a perfect awareness of what it means to be a member of a family on a universal scale. Our view is still too narrow: my fraternity, at most my Province, is the horizon. Joint activities and sharing of information are not yet felt as an urgency and a priority: we need to grow in this spirit of communion. I hope that this congress can be a privileged moment to build this communion. All the work of the commissions tends in this direction.

Let us now think of what Congress is proposing. You know that the Congress has a theme: Justice, Peace and Care of Creation. Certainly, with the help of the speakers, we want to sensitize the Laity to the urgency of this subject, but that is not the only reason we are here: we did not come to reflect on the various aspects of the life and mission of the lay fraternities of the Dominican Order. This is why you will be in various commissions to share, reflect and propose to the assembly paths for the next few years: it is your proposals that will be the richness of the assembly. The Laity is a branch of the Order called to live its independence, of course in communion with the Master of the Order and the Provincials, but as protagonists of their own life choices.

Your proposals will be voted on and I will present them to the Master of the Order for promulgation. This assembly must be the highest expression of the independence of the Laity and the expression of the full maturity of their Dominican vocation.

In the letter from the Master of the Order, which we have just heard, Bro. Bruno appeals to your ability to debate matters: that is, with respect and acceptance of other points of view. I am convinced that we will talk about situations of fracture in the Church; you know we feel that even in the various Episcopal Conferences: let us not be afraid of difference, it is a treasure, but please, always safeguard fraternal charity.

You know that we, the brothers and sisters here, are present to help you, but not to make decisions - that is your job. The proposals will be voted on by those who formally represent the provinces or countries.

How should we proceed in this work?

Each commission must find its own way of working: we do not have interpreters for the commissions, we only have them for the plenary sessions. I thank Sr Marie Théo, Sr Laetitia and Ruth Anne for this precious service. So each commission must find its way of working: to divide according to languages, etc. They must find a secretary who every day must meet with the other secretaries and with the general secretary. I ask you to write your texts on a computer: your text will be read and projected on the screen. The texts can be in French, Spanish and Italian.

The text, which should not be of more than 7 pages per commission, should have a preamble to frame the reflection, and short, precise sections so that we can identify what is significant and vote. We will vote section by section. Please take care: precise sections with concrete proposals.

We will have a motion presented by Belgium which must be discussed: this discussion must be prepared by the first commission.

We will vote section by section. Please give the texts to our interpreters as well. The richness of the congress depends on your shared reflections.

One more thing that is very important in the Dominican way of government: there will certainly be different views at the beginning, but after the vote, if the decision does not contradict the

Magisterium of the Church, it must be wholeheartedly accepted: it is the sense of consensus, so important in our Dominican vision. Well, we cannot propose or vote things that contradict the teaching of the Church. This point is very important: we will not say 'they decided' but 'we decided'; accepting the decisions of the assembly is an act of spiritual maturity.

I leave you a set of questions that I would like you to discuss in the commissions:

Broad topics for work in the commissions
1. Commission on Government, Rule and Statutes
   a) Analysis of the proposals of the Curia for the Rule and declarations of the Master of the Order.
   b) Evaluation of the structures of government: international council and regional councils and indications for their working.
   c) Welcoming people in special situations: divorced and remarried, people with different sexual orientations, etc.
   d) The meaning of the lay promise; which terminology would be most appropriate: profession, commitment etc.
   e) Search for lay language for fraternities: postulate, novitiate, change of name, etc., etc.
   f) External signs of belonging
2. Formation Commission
   a) Development of a formation plan for at least the first stage of formation
   b) Seek how to do formation at all levels: human, spiritual, theological, and formation for preaching. I am aware of a lack of formation specifically for preaching.
   c) The profile of the lay formation officer.

3. Communication and Finance Commission
   a) How to keep the database updated
   b) Participation in information at the general level
   c) Privacy policy and evaluation of content exchanged
   d) Financial collaboration of the fraternities: there should be a meeting of Promoters and religious assistants or formation officers and we cannot afford it. What can be done ?
4. Commission on the Dominican Family and Relations with the Local Church
   a) How we live the relationship with the other branches: meetings, shared mission, structures ...
   b) Recognition of fraternities in local churches
   c) Church delegation to preaching
5. Preaching and Spirituality Commission
   a) What lay preaching is. Lay models or clerical models
   b) Forms of preaching and urgency of preaching
   c) Preaching and fraternity
   d) A spiritual life that can feed this lay preaching
   e) Seeking a spirituality suited to lay life
   f) Formation on personal prayer
6. Justice and Peace Commission
   a) Provincial structures of justice and peace for the Laity
   b) How to engage the Laïcat in these areas of J and P
   c) Presence of J and P in the stages of formation
7. Promoters Commission
   a) The profile of Promoters and Religious Assistants
   b) Clarification of their functions
   c) Dialogue of the Provincial with the fraternities in the nomination of the Promoters and religious

assistants.

All this work will not be possible without a great openness to the Spirit of God. The discussions must be rooted in prayer: every day from 6.30 to 8.30 we will have Exposition of the Blessed Sacrament. You can freely spend a moment of personal prayer in the chapel. But you also have to have breakfast, so everyone must get organized to be prepared for Mass according to the shared program. This is prepared in fraternal meetings throughout the day: take the time to get to know other people, other realities, to build a Laity that is really a branch of the Order with fraternal links among those who live the same vocation.

Yesterday in Rome the Synod of Bishops on Youth began. The Holy Father urged the bishops to ardour and evangelical passion. In addition to reflecting on the relationship of the Fraternities with young people, I would also like us to reflect on this: this assembly should give us all the ardour and the evangelical passion that stirred St Dominic and the many Dominican male and female religious and lay people through the centuries and which one day inflamed us too.

And here in Fatima let us entrust all our concerns to the Virgin Mary, Mother of Preachers.

OPENING MESS - HOMILY

RUI MIGUEL ANGEL DEL RIO, O.P.
Octobre 4, 2018 – Feast of S. Francis

The holiness of the "poor man " of Assisi is characterized by an intense and universal light, capable of attracting the attention and desire of the heart towards the noblest aspects that our humanity is capable of expressing. The greeting that even today their friars, scattered all over the world, they direct to each person they encounter – "peace and all good " – briefly expresses a harmony found, with themselves, with others and with the world, that it is possible not only to experience but also to transmit to others. As Pope Francis recalled on his visit to Assisi at the beginning of his pontificate, this peace cannot be understood superficially, as a romantic inner peace:" Franciscan Peace is not a syrupy feeling. Please: this St Francis does not exist! And it's not even a kind of pantheistic harmony with the energies of the cosmos... Nor is this a Franciscan concept, but an idea that some have formed. The peace of Saint Francis is that of Christ, and it is found by the one who "takes on" his "yoke", which is to say his commandment: Love one another as I have loved you, (cf. John 13: 34; 15:12). And this "yoke" cannot be borne with arrogance, with presumption, with pride, but can only be carried with meekness and humility of heart (homily of Pope Francis, Piazza San Francesco, Assisi, October 4, 2013).

In any case, San Francisco himself could react to any reductive reading of his human and Christian experience with the words of St. Paul: "Brethren, far be it from me to glory except in the cross of our Lord Jesus Christ, by which the world has been crucified to me, and I to the world". (Gal 6: 14). The world that for the " little poor man" of Assisi was crucified is that medieval society – so far away and, at the same time, so close to ours – in which he was able to embody with determination all the poverty of spirit indicated by the Gospel of Christ until he was "a new creature" (6: 15). This path was not for Saint Francis a sudden simplification of living. Like any human being who is seriously measured against the "burning and sweet strength" of God's grace, Francis had to lose many battles with himself before he came to receive the Lord Jesus as the only Lord to serve, and from whom to learn the secret of a life that was poor, yet full of his natural need, to feel gratuitously loved: "All things have been committed to me by my Father. No one knows the Son except the Father, and no one knows the Father except the Son and those to whom the Son chooses to reveal him." (Mt 11, 27).

No one can accept to live the radical logic of the Beatitudes without having first understood the word of the Cross as the absolute, extreme manifestation of the love of God for every one of his creatures. On the other hand, you cannot experience this love except through a daily and incessant acceptance of your own and others' limits, which leaves in our bodies the mark of a lived alliance, until we can say without boasting: "I carry the marks of Jesus in my body" (Gal 6, 17). Francis experienced that living like this, taking on reality as the only place in which to be happy, and others as the only opportunity to love and be loved, transformed the weight of days into a sustainable lightness. With the delicate, unbreakable strength of the meek of heart, the "little poor man" ignited in the world and delivered to humanity the longing for an existence inspired by freedom and the joy of the Gospel, where the dream of fraternity is not impossible for those who find themselves willing trustingly to express their own need.

We end this reflection with the prayer of St. Francis for the world: "I pray you, then, my Lord Jesus Christ, Father of all mercy, not to remember our ingratitude, but bear in mind the inexhaustible clemency you have manifested, that it may always be the place and dwelling of those who truly know you and glorify your name, blessed and glorious, for ever and ever. Amen. "(Mirror of Perfection, 124; FF, 1824)

Different Aspect of the Formation in the Order

fr Vivian Boland, O.P.

Introduction

I am honoured to be invited to address the congress, I am very happy to be here, and I am happy also to share with you some thoughts about the different aspects of formation in the Dominican Order today.

As I am sure you know, a new *Ratio Formationis Generalis* for the friars was promulgated by the Master of the Order on 22 December 2016. This *Ratio* is a statute, or a set of norms and principles, which are given to the Order to guide the work of formation. For us that work is guided in the first place by the Constitutions and it is the Constitutions themselves that ask for a *Ratio Formationis Generalis*. They speak about it as follows (LCO 163):

> *There shall be a Ratio Formationis for the whole Order, approved by the general chapter or by the Master of the Order, and revised from time to time. It should lay down general spiritual principles and basic training norms for forming the brothers, leaving the*

provinces to develop their own norms as time and place demand.

It is to be revised from time to time, and because the previous version had been promulgated in 1987, the Jubilee Year of 2016 seemed like an appropriate time for a substantial revision of the *Ratio Formationis Generalis.*

I would like to speak about three things. In the first place I will say what is new about the *Ratio Formationis Generalis* of 2016 so as to see what are the aspects of formation that are given special emphasis today. Then I would like to say something about how the Dominican Laity might use the *Ratio* of the friars in thinking about their own formation. And finally, I want to refer to two recent letters of the Master of the Order which speak about the priorities for our mission today and specifically the role of the Dominican Laity in that mission. Formation is always for the mission of the Order and so in any particular place and time our formation must get some of its character and content from the missionary emphasis of that place and time. Because these letters of brother Bruno give direction for the Dominican mission today they ought also to guide our thinking about Dominican formation today.

THE 2016 RFG

If asked to identify what is new in the revised *Ratio Formationis Generalis* I pick out three things in particular.

There is an emphasis on the **role of the community** in the work of formation which was not present in the old *ratio*. When the new document speaks about those responsible for formation it speaks firstly of the community itself. The individual brother has his own special responsibility to develop his vocation and to live it as well as possible. He is helped by masters or formators who have responsibility for the novitiates and studentates of the Order. They in turn are helped by councils and chapters of the brothers, especially by formation councils established in each community of initial formation and for the province as a whole. But a place of priority is given to the formation community itself, so that everybody who is part of it is asked to share the responsibility of providing the best possible context for forming new brothers in the life and mission of the Order. In a recent symposium at Oxford about vocational discernment, a symposium that involved Benedictines, Jesuits and Dominicans, it was striking to see how much responsibility is given by our tradition to the chapters and councils of the communities when it comes to discerning and forming the new friars.

A second thing that is new, and in this the Order is simply thinking with the Church, is to consider **four basic aspects of formation**, the aspects of human formation, religious or spiritual formation, intellectual formation, and apostolic or pastoral formation. This distinction is first found, to the best of my knowledge, in *Pastores Dabo Vobis*, the apostolic exhortation from John Paul II in 1992 following a synod of bishops dedicated to priestly formation. But it has become common as a way of thinking about formation and we find it again in the most recent church document dedicated to priestly training, the *Ratio Fundamentalis Institutionis Sacerdotalis*, which was published in December 2016. One might debate some aspects of this distinction, and already I have been involved in a number of conversations in which certain aspects of it have been questioned. But it is a useful starting point, to consider formation in this holistic or integral way, involving these four aspects.

The third new element in our *Ratio Generalis* is that for the first time the Order has a ratio for **permanent formation** and not just for initial formation. This is another emphasis that is shared across the Church, a growing acceptance of the need for priests and religious – but we can add for all Christians too – to accept that discipleship means being forever in the school of Jesus. The Order was slow to accept this new emphasis. Earlier efforts at general chapters to give greater prominence to permanent formation were not successful. The chapters preferred to deal with it as a kind of appendix to initial formation. Many things have conspired to help us to change our minds about this, good things like a better understanding of human psychology and development, or a deeper appreciation of the challenges that come with the different stages and experiences of life, but also not so good things such as the sexual abuse crisis which is disturbing the Church so profoundly and which raises fundamental questions about human and spiritual maturity. So our recent general chapters have been happy to begin their consideration of formation by speaking about permanent formation and then seeing initial formation within that broader context. We are forever being formed in our following of Jesus and we are forever growing into our following of Dominic. It is not just aspects of our own nature and personality that require this. It is also the need to respond to changing situations and fresh challenges that come to anybody engaged in preaching the gospel today.

These are what I would pick out as the key new emphases of the 2016 *Ratio Generalis*: a stress on the role of the community in formation, a recognition of formation as holistic or integral involving human, spiritual, intellectual and apostolic aspects, and a recognition of the permanence of formation within which the years of initial formation have a special character but do not exhaust all that we must now say about formation.

THE NEW RATIO AND THE DOMINICAN LAITY

I hope that the new *Ratio Generalis* will not only be of interest to the Dominican Laity but will also be of help when you are thinking about your own formation. Our work of drafting a new *Ratio* was greatly facilitated by a very simple and clear statement with which the acts of the general chapter of Rome in 2010 began its consideration of formation (n.185):

> *The aim of our formation is the making of a Dominican preacher.*
> *Distinctive Dominican preaching must be the creative reference*
> *point of all other aspects of formation, human, spiritual,*

intellectual, and pastoral. The common zeal to share the fruits of contemplation of the Word of God provides the environment in which we all grow as preachers, a culture of mission.

So a first question, perhaps even a challenge, to yourselves is to ask how you would articulate the goal of your formation as Lay Dominicans? How would you express it? You might want to borrow from the sentences just quoted but you still need to qualify them in some way to bring out the specific character of your way of being Dominicans. What is the 'end product' that you wish, by God's grace, to be brought about through the work of formation? What kind of animal is the Lay Dominican? What are the characteristics of this animal when it is living well and flourishing as the kind of animal that it is? Your answers to those questions will already give you clear indications about what kind of formation you need to be thinking about.

When I quoted LCO 163 about the *Ratio Formationis Generalis* you will have noticed that it ends by saying that it is left to the provinces to develop their own norms as time and place demand. So in these years each province is engaged in producing a *Ratio Formationis Particularis* which adapts the general principles and fills out the basic structures of the *Ratio Generalis* for the context of each province.

Perhaps we could think of the Lay Dominicans doing something analogous to that. You could use the *Ratio Generalis* as a starting point but then adapt it, contextualise it and supplement it in accordance with your own particular way of living Dominican life and of participating in the Order's mission. An appendix to the *Ratio Generalis* gives guidelines for how a *ratio particularis* is to be drawn up. Decisions about certain matters are left to the discretion of each province. The general chapter of Bologna in 2016 also gave some guidelines for adapting the general principles and norms for formation to the needs of the individual provinces. It is interesting that these guidelines (AGC Bologna n.245) give special emphasis to the apostolic plan or 'community project' of each province. The process of formation needs to keep this provincial plan in mind and be established in such a way that the brothers being formed are being formed for the mission of the Order as it is contextualized in this or that part of the world.

So to continue the analogy, we can imagine the Lay Dominicans using the *Ratio Generalis* of the friars but adapting it to the apostolic plan or 'community project' of the fraternities. It would mean putting a second set of questions to yourselves, questions such as: what are the apostolic priorities of the lay fraternities in your province? How are the Lay Dominicans engaged in the life and mission of your province? How do we begin to contextualise the formation offered here or there in order to prepare Dominican laity well for their participation in the life and mission of a particular province?

It will also mean carrying through this reflection and revision of your formation programmes guided by the new emphases which I spoke about under the first point: the place of the community in formation, the different aspects of formation if it is to be integral, and the fact that we are asked now to think always in terms of permanent formation and not just of initial formation.

PRIORITIES FOR MISSION AND FORMATION TODAY

So for what mission, for what project, are lay Dominicans being formed today? What are the current priorities and preoccupations of the Order for help with which it looks to its lay members? I suggest that we find a very good answer to these questions in two recent letters of the Master of the Order, his letter after the Mission Congress which brought the Jubilee celebrations to an end, and his letter to the Dominican laity in preparation for this congress in which we are now participating. The first letter is dated 25 March 2017 and the second is dated 25 January 2018. How are lay Dominicans to be formed today for the Order of Preachers whose mission is currently orientated in the ways indicated after the Mission Congress? How are lay Dominicans to be formed today so as to respond to the challenges shared with you by the Master in his letter in preparation for this Fatima Congress?

When the goal is clear it becomes easy to talk about the human, spiritual, intellectual and apostolic formation that is required to achieve it. This is what the general chapter of Rome helped us to do in relation to our formation as friars of the Order. My proposal, humbly submitted, is that the Laity should undertake a similar exercise. Your formation, both initial and permanent, should prepare you to take your place in the mission of the Order as it is conceived today. In order to do that your formation, both initial and permanent, needs to be guided by the goals and priorities outlined in these two letters from brother Bruno.

From the Mission Congress

The letter after the Mission Congress summarised all that had been presented during the days of the Congress and identified three main convictions that had emerged about the Order's mission today: a conviction about **preaching**, a conviction about **fraternity**, and a conviction about **encounter**. These are some central guiding realities to inform any fresh thinking about formation and they come not just from the Master of the Order but from the more than six hundred members of the Dominican family who took part in the Mission Congress and whose work the Master summarised in his letter. Remember that the largest single group at the Congress were the lay members of the Order.

So preaching, fraternity and encounter. A focus on preaching is not a surprise for an Order whose heart is given to the loving service of the Word of God. But the Mission Congress did not wish simply to re-assert the Order's central mission but to identify those aspects of it that need renewal among us: a lifestyle that supports preaching, a generous, courageous and creative service of the Word, a concern for the different languages in which we are called to communicate about the Word (language meaning also things like music and art).

The focus on fraternity was particularly on the experience of friendship which we carry for the Church and for the world, a friendship being strengthened between us on the basis of the friendship of God that is the subject matter of our preaching: God's friendship towards us, God's call to us to share in the friendship that he is, the life we share together as friends of the Bridegroom, calling others to come and share in the joy of our Lord.

And encounter is the form our preaching must take, today more than ever, following the example of Jesus and Dominic as we see them meeting people, listening, questioning, giving time and attention, staying with people as they face their difficulties and as they search for truthful ways of living. One of the most powerful moments of the Mission Congress was that dedicated to reflecting on Jesus' conversations with the Samaritan woman in John 4 and with the disciples on the road to Emmaus in Luke 24.

Preaching, fraternity, encounter: we learn these things in the first place from God's way of communicating his Word to us, from God's way of bringing us into His friendship, from God's way of establishing and sustaining dialogue in His encounter with His people. The Mission Congress also presented us with many experiences of restlessness, of communities, places and situations where people are restless and to which we are particularly called to speak a word of healing, reconciliation, peace and mercy, to be preachers of grace in all those ways. The world needs the Word that builds communion and the work of preaching the Word of God's grace is inseparable from the work of building communion. As his letter unfolds, the Master speaks about the importance for this of theology, the need for fresh study to which our preaching will inevitably send us and from which we are then sent back to preaching. He speaks of permanent formation, already mentioned. He speaks of the Order as a family in the heart of the Church, a point to which I shall return. He speaks of moving forward in the mission of the Order while doing so in the path of tradition, handing on to a new generation what we ourselves have received. And he speaks about the Salamanca process, an approach which asserts very clearly the human dignity of all persons and which works to defend and promote that dignity, and the rights that go with it, particularly in situations where these are under threat.

Finally the Master comes to some concrete priorities for the Order's mission today: the worlds of young people, digital culture, migration, and study as a mission of the Order.

It might seem as if I have asked the Master to write my talk for me! But what I want to stress is the importance of aligning our formation, both initial and permanent, with the apostolic concerns of the Order of Preachers today. The aspects of formation being underlined in the Church and in the Order are those I mentioned earlier – the role of the community or fraternity, the need for permanent formation considering our own development in response to the changing demands being made on us, and the need for a holistic or integral formation that will take account not just of religious and intellectual aspects but of the human and the apostolic aspects as well. The letter after the Mission Congress articulates the mission of the Order as it is understood by us today and the formation of all branches of the Order ought to be guided by that articulation.

Towards the International Congress 2018

The letter of brother Bruno to the laity of the Order in preparation for this Congress makes concrete for the Dominican laity the challenges and priorities already identified for the whole Order. Not surprisingly the first place is given to the **sign of fraternity**. This is a first task for the mission and therefore for the formation of lay Dominicans also. You are to be a sign in the world that humans carry within them the ability to live as brothers and

INTERNATIONAL COUNCIL OF LAY DOMINICAN FRATERNITIES

sisters. Within the fraternities you are called to establish relations which, even with all your diversity, unite you in the same relationship with God and in the same desire to be sent as witnesses of the Word of life and grace.

Another term we must use is the term **family**. We are accustomed to speaking of the Dominican family in order to include all the branches that belong in some way to the Order of Preachers. It is even more specific in your case because many, though not all, lay Dominicans live their vocation in the context of family life, as husbands or wives, as fathers or mothers. Pope Francis has spoken often about the gospel of the family and how the family is to be an agent of evangelization. This is something the Order looks to you to teach the rest of us, how the life of families can be supported and strengthened through your membership of the Order and how families in their ordinary reality can be bearers of the grace of the Lord and witnesses in the world to that grace.

Continuing the theme of preaching as **encounter and dialogue**, there are many places and situations other than family life itself, that are accessible to the lay brothers and sisters of the Order in ways that they are not accessible to the friars, nuns or sisters. Brother Bruno speaks about how the lay Dominicans are in the front line in many areas of professional life, where important issues of ethics, justice and meaning arise. In medicine and law, in communications and ecology, in education and business: in all cases there are encounters with people, there is working together, there is a shared search for meaning, truth and goodness. Some of the questions that arise in these areas will send us back to study, to learn more and to understand more about the many questions humanity is facing and about the light to be shed on these questions from the Word of God. From our tradition we can engage with these concerns and make a contribution to finding solutions for them.

Ecumenical and interreligious dialogue is an area of particular importance which gets special mention in the Master's letter. Because of your immediate and daily contact and interaction with people of other faiths and religious beliefs, lay Dominicans are on the front line in this matter also in ways that other members of the Dominican family are not.

The **worlds of youth** get special mention, a point that had already been emphasised in the Mission Congress. The Synod of Bishops devoted to this is just beginning in Rome and it is a moment to renew our commitment to promoting the participation of young people in the preaching mission of the Order. One particular issue that needs to be thought about is how to facilitate the transition of younger people from the various youth groups attached to the Order to a lifelong participation in the lay fraternities of the Order.

Returning at the end of his letter to the question of the family, brother Bruno speaks about the welcome, discernment and accompaniment needed where lay brothers and sisters are in irregular situations. It is a question that has exercised the whole Church since the last two synods on the family and it is one that arises in many of the lay fraternities. How are we to honour the reality of being signs of fraternity in a world and in a Church that are marked by brokenness and imperfection? How are we to be preachers of grace and mercy not just in word but also in practice? Brother Bruno made a specific request to all the provincial officials of the Dominican Laity about this. From the point of view of my theme, aspects of formation in the Dominican Order, you can see once again the need for permanent formation in order to understand well, to respond well and to continue building the signs of fraternity that we want to be.

CONCLUSION

To conclude: the formation of the Lay Dominican in the way of Saint Dominic needs to be integral, a formation in human, religious, intellectual and apostolic maturity. It needs to be permanent, a formation that builds constantly on what was received in the time of initial formation. And it needs to be undertaken in community since it is the community that confirms the promptings of the Holy Spirit in the hearts of each one.

I have stressed that it is a formation for the mission of the Order because the end of the Order is an apostolic one: we are all at the service of the proclamation of the Word of God, to evangelise in the world the name of Jesus Christ. Lay Dominicans have a particular role and contribution in this mission. They are formed by and for life in the family, in the Order, in the Church, and in the world. Having their own experience of these different circles of life – the family, the Order, the Church, the world – lay Dominicans are in a very good place from which to allow each of these circles to illuminate the others.

In this third part of my talk I have presented the main lines of the Order's understanding of its mission today. I have done so because our formation is always for our mission. So my final question to you is this: how can the Order best help and equip you, through the initial and permanent formation it offers you, to play your part in responding to these contemporary challenges?

ECOLOGY AND CARE OF CREATE – PART 1

Lissette A. Avilés-Ríos, Op

Good morning, I extend to you an eco-friendly greeting, a renewable blessing and a sustainable embrace. I thank the organizers, especially Héctor Márquez, for the invitation to accompany them in this third International Congress.

The theme or reflection that I will share, I have developed from three moments or three glances. These "glances " are simply the way the Church in Latin America and the Caribbean approaches the reality through seeing, judging and acting; and which from integral ecology we call it the three glances: lovingly to see reality with its lights and shadows; carefully to judge in the light of the Word of God, the documents of the Magisterium and any other document that carefully helps to arouse the third glance, namely to act/hopefully.

The first glance will be an invitation to see or look lovingly at the place where we are, where we came from, simply, to see the reality of our planet. The second glance or second moment, will be to take a careful look at creation through the lenses of the encyclical *Laudato Sí*. And a third moment will be an invitation to a hopeful look at our Dominican spirituality to achieve an integral ecology that helps in the care of creation.

LET'S TAKE OUR FIRST LOOK

I invite you to recall something from your place of origin and remember some landscape or place that you like very much; you have three seconds for this (pause of three seconds). Then remember your journey here to Fatima, and try to recall some landscape that drew your attention; you have three more seconds (three-second pause). Now you have one minute to share in a soft voice or to "cuchichear" (as we say in Puerto Rico), with the person next to you, these places or landscapes of which you like or which attract your attention. (one-minute pause)

I hope that before you share the favorite landscape and if you didn't know the person next to you, you asked her/his name or you have introduced yourselves. Moreover, I wonder if the images or landscapes you shared, which are your favorites, included people or were just trees, birds, mountains, the sea, a river... And it is very natural that faced with an exercise like this, we only think of a beautiful landscape, without people or buildings. My favorite place is the following (image of the Bay of St. John, with in the background part of the old Saint John, seen from Catanho, specifically, the convent where I live, Saint Vincent Ferrer Convent).

Now, I invite you to ask yourselves if your relationship with God, according to the Dominican charism and spirituality, is reflected in dealing with other people, whether believers or not, is reflected in the way you deal with yourself, and is reflected in how you treat and how you take care of your environment. In other words, if I had the opportunity to walk with you, without being seen, could I see your love and relationship with God reflected in the way you relate to yourself, to others and to your environment?

Going back to your favorite places, it is common to think of natural landscapes, excluding people or buildings, believing that speaking of ecology only refers to what is created by God.

This term, ecology, is credited to the zoologist, Ernst Haeckel, who as early as 1869 used it to refer to the interrelationships of organisms with their environment or their surroundings. If we look up the origin of 'ecology', it comes from the Greek word *oikos* meaning home. Today, this concept has

been extended to all manifestations of life or the biosphere. What is meant by biosphere or life is that it is composed of a diversity of ecosystems/systems of homes that interact with each other. And here it includes us as human beings, so it's worth asking, how do we relate to our environment with our *oikos*, with our home?

In this Loving Glance (and "loving" means the ability to see reality with its lights and shadows; the loving glance like that of a father or mother when they speak of their sons and daughters. He or she knows how much "good " or how "terrible " their child is, but still does not cease to love him or her), we must acknowledge the reality of our great *Oikos*/home, or as Pope Francis encourages us to call it, Our Shared Home. Let's look at some data from Our Shared Home, some realities that are suffered or experienced in some rooms or regions or countries. I can tell you that when I hear the words Shared Home, I cannot help but imagine the planet as a house of several floors or levels, or an immense house, like a mansion with a diversity of rooms. Each room represents a country. But let us look at some realities of this Home and, above all, how we act in it...

In 2014, the World Fund for Nature reported that in the first 8 months of that year, 2014, human beings "consumed " or used the natural resources that the planet takes a year to produce. And they announced that human beings, with the current lifestyle, with accelerated technological changes, by the year 2050 or perhaps before, will need three planets to supply their "apparent needs ". I use the expression "apparent needs" because if we look at the proportion of those who are "Christians " in the world, no matter to which denomination we belong, we are one-third of the world's population. And one assumes that a Christian chooses and distinguishes him- or herself by having a simple life, in the style of the Master, of our Lord Jesus Christ: hence the title of Christian, or "another Christ ". This does not include the large number of people who have had a basis of Christian faith and who are now agnostics or belong to another religion, and I hope that something good has been inherited from our faith.

In 2017, it was recorded that human beings had generated an approximate total of 10 billion tons of garbage since 2012. This means that, daily in those five years, we generated 228,000 tonnes per hour and that three0% of these waste materials were not collected or dealt with. Lest we forget, the decomposition times: a plastic bag takes 150 years to decompose, batteries about 1000 years to decompose (think of all that we, the Puerto Ricans, had to use in the last year because of the loss of electric energy, due to the impacts of the hurricanes Irma and Maria), and glass or crystal take about 4000 years. There is an Internet page, "Waste Atlas ", where the production of garbage is recorded per country. Without doubt, we can say, as Pope Francis did in §21: "The earth, our home, is beginning to look more and more like an immense pile of filth." Of course, the most developed "rooms" or countries generate a greater amount of garbage or waste. In addition, these waste materials will sometimes end up in the less developed areas or countries, or the raw material is extracted from them. The effect of production of these waste materials affects climate change, for they are not only plastic, metals, paper, but also gases that produce the greenhouse effect, which raises the temperature of our Home. Not to mention that many of these residues do not remain in any "room", but end up in the courtyard of the whole Common Home, the ocean, where floating islands of garbage are already recorded. I urge you to watch the documentary, *A Plastic Ocean*.

Pope Francis is right to emphasize that in the world there are not two crises, environmental and social or human, but a single socio/environmental crisis. What is harmful to nature redounds on society, especially on the most vulnerable, and vice versa, what affects society has repercussions on the environment, whether we realise it or not.

SECOND LOOK: JUDGING CAREFULLY

What I have outlined is very brief, but "as proof, one example is enough," as they say. With these data, I am trying, as the Pope does in *Laudato Si* §19: "to become painfully aware, to dare to turn what is happening to the world into our own personal suffering and thus to discover what each of us can do about it." Lifestyle changes are urgent, not only among Catholic Christians, but throughout the entire human race.

Laudato Si is directed to all people, believers and non-believers, so that we acknowledge that the planet is Our Common Home, the Home of the human being and of every creature, small as it is and although we barely realise that it exists. That the planet Earth is our Mother, our Sister. I know that there are people, Dominicans from about three9 countries, who have chosen a simple life, either because their culture helps them to maintain a connection with creation or because their conversion process, accompanied as they are by the spirit of Saint Dominic de Guzman, encourages them. In their search for truth, they contemplate the creation as a whole, and are aware of the interconnectivity that exists between the human being and creation. These people are able to read the history of salvation that is updated day by day in nature and see themselves as part of it and not superior to it.

But we cannot deny that there are others to whom, possibly, our Christianity and Dominicanism do not reflect this love or this relationship of respect to God, to others or to the environment in the same way.

When I find people who in their way of acting do good both to other human beings and to nature, I cannot but recognise that the

Gospel of Creation is made clear. What do I mean by the Gospel of Creation? It is none other than the ability to interpret the what is written in Genesis, which speaks to us of the creation of our world and of human beings, not feeling like the owners and lords of all that the Creator has given them. On the contrary, they acknowledge with their responsible actions that the care of what is created by God is the task of the Believer, who are caregivers of creation or, as some call it, administrators of creation.

I think of our Father Saint Dominic. It is said that he spoke to God or about God, and that in one of his ways of prayer, in which he integrated the body with the spirit, he contemplated and integrated the creation to bear the fruit of what he contemplated. What would he tell us today, about the reality of Our Common Home? How would you describe God, in what you contemplate in creation? It is curious, in the iconography with our Father founder there is a dog, symbol of fidelity, with the torch in its mouth to illuminate the world. I wonder, what will be the iconography of each of those present here? What animal or element would you use to describe us in order to reflect hope in the world?

Let me share with you what my life sign is, not because I am exactly like them, but they help me to be a better human being and a better Christian. My sign is the sea turtle. Because they are turtles, they are considered slow, influenced by the tale of "The hare and the tortoise." And yes, they are slow outside their environment, but anyone who has had the opportunity to see them in the sea, knows that it's not easy to keep up with them when they are swimming. All they need are a few fins and they leave us behind with ease. Their slowness emerges when, after passing through the process of fertilization, the female goes to the edge of some beach, which she possibly visited at other times and where there is no contamination of artificial light, to lay her eggs. When she comes out of the water, her weight makes her move slowly, but steadily. On reaching the proper level of the beach, she will twirl round and with her rear fins start digging a hole almost one meter deep. When she feels that the nest is deep enough and safe, she will start laying the first eggs slowly, until a moment comes when she becomes "ecstatic". She knows that this moment has come, because her eyes begin to water and that is the moment of complete dedication, and is when scientists can approach to measure them or identify them. Nothing and no one will interrupt her in your process of giving up her fruits.

Once she has laid all her eggs, she will cover the nest with sand and slowly begin her return to the sea. After a few months, the young will come out of their eggs, finding the way out to the surface from the small bag of air which forms inside the egg and which shows how to get out of the nest. Once on the surface they will begin their venture to the sea. Their mother will not meet them on the coast, but after several years, they may share the very beach where it all began.

I recognize that in my life, I have had moments of great agility, strength, security, and that happens when I am in my own environment, in these pastoral experiences working with people, giving the fruit of what I have contemplated. But... I also recognize the moments when I was moving slowly. These moments when the experience with God and with others drive me to leave my comfort zone in order to give of my best, to bear witness to the experience of God in my life amid the difficulties. These experiences where I had to look into my life and see how far they reflect the project of the Kingdom. On other occasions, I had to dig very deep to make life possible, at those times when complete trust in God is what sustains me. There, where the itinerancy takes shape and after doing what I had to do, I left for another place, without necessarily seeing or understanding the fruits of the mission and starting again to contemplate life. I am grateful that God the Father/Mother created sea turtles and has put his wisdom in them, to teach me.

THIRD GLANCE: ACT HOPEFULLY

Is it worth asking ourselves how our spirituality and charism can contribute to caring for God's creation, both human beings and nature? To this end, we must apply several "R "s that drive us in integral ecology. The best known are recycling, reusing, re-gathering, rebuilding, among many others. But there is one that in my view must be paramount, and that is rethinking.

Rethinking the lifestyle we have to adopt or opt for. Not only as regards the economic aspect of the question of achieving a simpler lifestyle, but recognizing that we have no other planet, that there do not exist or are not available three more planets whose annual production can be used in less than a year. That we are responsible for other generations being able to enjoy this Common Home and make possible the project of the Kingdom.

Rethinking at the time of buying a product, whatever it may be, and identifying the use we will make of it, if buying it is justified in terms of the expenditure of energy it will entail. Rethink who we're affecting so that we can enjoy this product.

Rethinking the use of fossil fuels used to travel from one place to another, or to produce energy. When we commit ourselves to rethinking, we realize that there are other possible kinds of energy and we will be able to demand that our governments opt for these.

Rethinking that the water coming out of the tap, which starts as drinking water, the water that can be ingested, is the same that is used in most places to wash clothes, plates and cutlery, to flush the lavatory, to wash cars... And we should not forget the number of people and organizations for whom it is becoming increasingly difficult to access this element that nourishes life.

Rethinking how to integrate the theme of the care of creation within the formation, the prayer, the life of the community and the mission. It is urgent for us to collaborate in this Common Home to discover the truth hidden in every creature, to discover the wisdom that God has placed in his creation in order to live our Dominican humanity in line with it.

Rethinking how to continue cultivating the ability to contemplate the truth beyond books, perhaps as our father did, who, when he contemplated hunger in his time, sold his books to give life. Let us rethink what hunger is today: hunger for the meaning of life, the hunger of the existential emptiness that leads us to fill it with things and takes us away from what is simple in life. It is this quest to fill this emptiness, which distances us from seeing God reflected in the other human being, distances us from seeing God in everything created.

In these days, I had the opportunity to contemplate the greatness and importance of Dominican spirituality for the Church and for our Common Home. And looking for an image that would help to make and animate our preaching mission, I recently shared a reflection with a group of fathers and mothers of families in a chapel near the village where I live, contemplating with

them our brother coral. For all those of us who live in tropical or subtropical coastal areas, we know how valuable and important coral is; also, how fragile and susceptible to temperature changes and how it is affected by contamination or sediments. But let us draw near to what they are and what we can learn from them.

The first thing is to recognize that corals are animals and not plants, in addition to living in community or collectively. Their growth is estimated at 1.5 cm per year, yes, slow growth, but each time they grows, it is not that each organism becomes larger in itself, but that the volume of calcium in it increases. It is this rock that is beneath it and that by keeping coral healthy, forms a natural barrier that has several functions.

1. It serves as a barrier or breaks the waves, which helps to protect the coasts from erosion before the battering or the powerful energy of the swell or of the tides.

2. It serves as habitat or home for other organisms by creating the reefs, providing them with safety and food.

Now imagine Saint Dominic as the first organism that sought to form community and that after more than 800 years, created and left the formation of reefs in many places of our Common Home. Leaving a footprint of how to live the Gospel of the Kingdom. And yes, we had moments of difficulty, of challenges, of discouragement, but still, Dominican spirituality has been home for many, safety for others, food for all.

May our spirituality and charism make us rethink and opt for an evangelical style and may we express it with consistent words and actions. So may God and St Dominic de Guzmán help us to continue interceding for the Dominican family. A supportive embrace and renewable blessings. Thank you!

ECOLOGY AND CARE OF CREATE – PART 2

Aristide Basse, OP

INTRODUCTION

I am very happy to speak here on the occasion of the Third International Congress of Lay Dominicans here in Fatima, Portugal. Many thanks for the invitation to Br Rui Carlos, Promoter General of Dominican Laity, to take part in this global mass and to speak on the subject "Ecology and care of creation". In our time the world is crisscrossed by problems, both recent and current. Among them is the problem of climate change which involves every human being, every politician, every Christian. As to Christians, I would say that their faith involves them in their relationship with the Earth, for their whole lives.

Pope Francis' promulgation of *Laudato Si'*, the very first papal encyclical devoted to environmental and ecological problems (24 May 2015), shows the importance and the necessary consideration of the Earth as our "common home" at the heart of the pastoral concern of the "Pope of the poor" who wants a Church "for the poor". For the Holy Father, there are so to speak two imperatives for the Church, indeed for the world today: the environment and the poor. This theme runs throughout the very first encyclical of a Pope on the environment, our "common home". He told us in his Tweet on 14 November 2013: "Take care of the Earth, but above all take care of those people who do not have what is necessary to live". Here is a challenge with two dimensions for today's world, a single challenge with two intrinsically connected links. And all this may be called Life. Now, this life is what challenges the imperative, unavoidable technoscience of our times.

The Church is concerned about the environment and climate change because it is a question of life, and the Church must promote and protect life as a gift of God. Everything that is said about the environment and climate change is closely linked with human life. Pope Francis says that the Earth is our "common home"[1]. It is a matter of relationship and interrelationship between Man and the world, between man and creation, between Man and the planet. And if the common home is affected, human life is affected. It is the Church's concern with human life that drives her to promote environmental education.

Our talk will turn on three great points:
- the worldwide ecological crisis
- Christianity, participant in the ecological crisis?
- A Christian ethics and spirituality of creation

I: THE WORLDWIDE ECOLOGICAL CRISIS

The ecological crisis is a very present-day worldwide matter and problem above all in this technological civilisation. And we know that the problem of ecology, of the environment is linked to other domains of human life, which is why it cries out to various

---

[1] In *Laudato Si'*, the first ever encyclical by a Sovereign Pontiff essentially and totally dedicated to ecological questions, Pope Francis portrays all the disasters on the Earth, our sister and our mother.

participants in political, intellectual and religious life. We are going to think seriously about this crisis. First we will analyse the danger in the world.

THE WORLD IN DANGER

"The world in danger" is the very first sight that reveals present-day life to us. It offers us poignant examples that we experience and that really show us that life has changed and is threatened on Earth because of Man's own actions. The risk Man is running comes more form technology as unavoidable for human life today. Many facts testify to this danger that threatens the existence of the world, of humanity. Thus Man must face a "fundamental challenge".

Let us recall the explosion of the nuclear reactor in Chernobyl which sounded the alarm on this danger in 1986. The consequences were disastrous. Afterwards, for NASA (the USA's National Aeronautics and Space Administration) "the year 1988 proved to be a pivotal year in ecological awareness and public opinion"[2], because of the reality of global warming which testifies to this danger. Nor do we forget the catastrophe of Fukushima in Japan.

The other facet of danger comes from the reality of poverty. This is what emerges from the Report of the World Commission on the Environment and Development, known as the *Rapport Brundtland*. Poverty that reveals a lack drives Man to actions that may be harmful for him, because man seeks prosperity. As it is like a global calamity, it also causes hardship when there is the desire to eradicate it. Poor countries desperately set upon their soil with practices that destroy and drain them. This makes them still poorer or makes their survival ever more precarious. In reality, the third-world countries use oppressive manoeuvres on their environment in

---

[2] *"l'année 1988 s'est révélée une année charnière dans la prise de conscience écologique et l'opinion publique"*, in René COSTE, *Dieu et l'écologie : Théologie, environnement, spiritualité*, Paris, Atelier, 1994, p. 20.

order to survive; think, for example, of slash-and-burn culture or deforestation.

The developed countries rob the poor countries of their land for their own benefit; and yet these poor tracts of land do not, for that matter, even help the poor countries. For instance, in the countries south of the Sahara the catastrophes scream out that "the relationships between attacks on the environment and the collapse of development appear all the more brutally"[3]. In fact, the manner of development initiated by the Northern countries and which for the most part are "destroyers" of the sub-Sahara environmental space (because of the history of colonisations) drive the people to put less profitable pressure on this vital space.

Among the various dangers that threaten the world we may also not the difficulties arising from the imbalance between the powerful demographic surge and the increase in production. The more numerous the people become, the more must be produced, "nutrients" are required to feed them. Hence the large world population leads to still more exploitation of the resources of the Earth. Now, this population is increasing enormously. So there is greater need for natural resources. Among our exploitations is a politics that favours the non-regeneration of our resources. When we talk of regeneration, we think of *biocapacity* and of the *ecological footprint*[4]. The Canadians Mathis Wackernagel and William Reese use *ecological footprint* to express the rate at which we consume natural resources and produce waste. As for *biocapacity*, it is the rate at which nature can absorb waste and generate new resources. We may think of the balance between the *ecological footprint* and *biocapacity*, rather

---

[3] "*les relations entre les agressions contre l'environnement et la faillite du développement apparaissent le plus brutalement*", ibid., p.22

[4] Jean-Marie GUEULETTE and Fabien REVOL (eds.), *Avec les créatures. Pour une approche chrétienne de l'écologie,* Parie, Cerf, 2015, p. 138-139. Lire aussi A. BOUTAUD and N. GONDRAN, *L'empreinte écologique,* Paris, Ed. La Découverte, 2009. The ecological footprint expressed in the unit of measurement called 'global hectare" (hag) is intended to measure the real influence of human activity on the Earth.

than there being a heavy weight of *biocapacity* on the *ecological footprint*.

Climate change as a result of the rise in temperature results largely from human activities. To talk of climate change is to talk of greenhouse gases and of "additional" gases that arise from human activities with technological support. To speak of the not negligible place of human activities in the ecological crisis, scientists have invented the concept "anthropocene", a new era into which humanity has entered and which is characterised by the negative impacts of human acts on the atmosphere, the environment , the planet. Entering the anthropocene, it is human beings themselves that threaten nature, the environment, their own living space – in a word, they threaten themselves. We have reached the limit beyond which we must not go.

All the dramatic situations our world is experiencing are pathological signs of an existence that is proving to be precarious and, so to speak, hanging by a thread: "humanity is in danger". Hence the appeals of philosophers, intellectuals and theologians to an awareness and to the adoption of responsible behaviour for the life of humanity bound to that of nature, of the environment. Various ethics are being proposed.

II – CHRISTIANITY, PARTICIPANT IN THE ECOLOGICAL CRISIS[5]

To speak more clearly about the ecological crisis at its origin, we believe that it is necessary to make an approach through the definition of the term ecology. Its coiner and initiator was a German biologist, Ernst Haeckel, populariser of the ideas of Darwin, who in 1866 wrote: "By Ecology, we mean the totality of the science of the relationships of the organism with its environment, including in the

---

[5] Christianity is accused of having favoured the ecological crisis the world is experiencing. We wish to stress that in part these ecological criticisms were for an anti-Christian ecology.

broad sense all the conditions of existence"[6]. We can see that what is at the heart of the discipline of ecology is relationship. In fact, ecology studies the interrelationships between the various organisms and their environment.

We know that Christianity has been accused of being at the origin of the ecological crisis that the industrial world is experiencing. The initial helping hand was given by the American Lynn White Jr., who on 26 December 1966, relying on the command "Be fruitful and multiply, and fill the earth and subdue it; and have dominion over the fish of the sea and over the birds of the air and over every living thing that moves upon the earth" (Genesis 1:28), reproved Christianity for "what it calls its anthropocentrism, which, according to it, makes Man not only the privileged creature, but also the absolute master of our planet earth and the centre of the universe. It is reckoned that Christianity, above all in its western version, is the most anthropocentric religion in the world"[7].

It is a matter of a presumed rupture which it supposedly introduced between Nature and Man, making it possible for the latter to set himself against Nature: this is how the upholders of a profound, authentic ecology, antichristian ecology, see the ecological crisis. To answer this criticism launched against Christianity or rather Judaeo-Christian thinking demands that we proceed by way of a theology of creation that is based on a meticulous biblical analysis.

OF THE REALITY OF THE CREATOR GOD AND OF MAN AS MANAGER

In order to answer the accusation against Christianity, suspected of being at the origin of environmental devastation, Fr

---

[6] "*Par Ökologie, nous entendons la totalité de la science des relations de l'organisme avec son environnement, comprenant au sens large toutes les conditions d'existence*" in R. MILLER, *Ecologie*, translation of the 4th éd., Brussels, de Boeck et Glacier, 2005, p. XIX.

[7] René COSTE, *op.cit.*, p. 43.

René Coste is summoned: he moves from the theology of creation, an indispensable path for truly understanding Man's place in the heart of all creation his responsibility towards the created universe. It is God who created everything and entrusted to Man (likewise created) a mission that must be taken on reasonably, responsibly to respect Him to whom he must report.

God the Creator

The Old Testament offers us two accounts of the creation. And in the Apostles' Creed and the liturgical thinking of Nicea-Constantinople, we confess that God created Heaven and Earth, what is visible and what is invisible. The theory of creation *ex nihilo* states that God created everything starting from nothing. He did not have recourse to any pre-existing material to carry out his work. The Omnipotent God is Creator in the full sense of the term. The totality of the real or of the universe comes from God, the *Pantokrator*.

Man in the image of God: Manager of creation

To speak of God as Creator also sends us back to the outstandingly important consideration of creatures. We know that Man (male and female humanity) was made in the image (*selem*) and likeness (*demût*) of God. Man as Imago Dei is such in his entirety (in his material and spiritual totality). The creation of Man placed at the end of the process of creation underlines the pre-eminence of Man in relation to the other creatures: it is he who gives each of them a name, which is a way of showing his superiority[8]. But this does not mean that he should distance himself from the other creatures[9].

God entrusted a mission to Man: to watch over all creation. The

---

[8] On this, see Olivier LANDRON, *Le Catholicisme vert. Histoire des relations entre l'Église et la nature au xxe siècle,* Paris, Éditions du Cerf, coll. «Histoire», 2008, pp. 66-74.

[9] Creation is a factor of communion between God and all creation; a factor of communion between Man and the other creatures, hence with Nature: the original harmony between Man and other created beings, man living in an original justice.

Bible tells us: And God blessed them, and God said to them, "Be fruitful and multiply, and fill the earth and subdue it; and have dominion over the fish of the sea and over the birds of the air and over every living thing that moves upon the earth" (Gen. 1:28). Two verbs are important in this mission[10]: God took Man and put him in the garden to "cultivate and keep it". In Hebrew, the verbs cultivate (*avad*) and keep (*shamar*) have a religious connotation: we keep the commandments of God; to cultivate or work is to give worship to God, to serve God. So cultivating is serving God. Every priest who has to keep (guard) the sanctuary must preserve it from any act of defilement. In a similar sense, Man must protect the Earth from any destruction. As we see, the ecological criticism of White Lynn and of those who hold theories against anthropocentrism is founded on a misinterpretation of the mission entrusted to Man. Man is in fact a manager. We know that management has an essential double dimension: on the one hand, it means the Man is not the owner, and so there is a limit to the power of humanity; on the other hand there is a field of creative freedom, of inventiveness on the part of Man. Thus Man faced with creation must take creative, inventive, ameliorative initiatives, knowing all the while that he is only an administrator, he has to report back. In fact, creation is, so to speak, the Garden of God where Man is the gardener, the one who cultivates in order that it may bear fruit[11].

Psalm 8 shows us the glorifying, very beneficial power of Man over creation, over our planet. The book of Sirach is also full of the sense of responsible, intelligent, provident power of Man over creation (17:1-14). In all the wisdom literature, the most noteworthy text, in effect a compendium of this doctrine of beneficent, responsible, provident, thoughtful power of Man over the universe

---

[10]Cf. René COSTE, op.cit., p. 66.

[11] We know that in order to improve the garden, the gardener loves it and procures everything necessary to make it productive. God, who created Man to be his opposite, established him as partner. HENCE man is bound to collaborate with God.

is from the Book of Wisdom: "O God of my ancestors and Lord of mercy, who have made all things by your word, and by your wisdom have formed humankind to have dominion over the creatures you have made, and rule the world in holiness and righteousness,and pronounce judgment in uprightness of soul" (9:1-3). This prayer implicitly tells us of the behaviour Man must adopt towards the created universe. It is his power that man must exercise for the wellbeing of the universe, but also for his own sanctification.

The destructive exploitation of nature would be an injustice towards Nature herself and a sin before God but also against the other inhabitants.

THE PROHIBITION IN RELATION TO THE MANAGEMENT OF CRÉATION

Scripture, Tradition and the Magisterium put us in the position of clearing the name of Man, Imago Dei, made and advised to control creation and not serve it to serve God. We are going to look again at certain Old Testament texts and at the thinking of some modern religious leaders to explain the fact that industrialisation, at the same time as secularisation, or dechristianisation, is what ravages the world and controls Man and creation.

Law of the Sabbath, the law of uncultivated land and the human right to sustenance

Rereading and recontextualising Genesis 1, we see that the creation of all beings comes to an end with God's resting. This rest, called Shabbat – for Christians today, Sunday – shows that God the Creator who creates by working and works by creating, and who gives power to Man to dominate the non-human environment (land and animals), wants Man to let the land rest too. Working to seek his maintenance of *dominium terrae*, man the "landowner" must allow it to rest. The land, like the Creator needs to rest. One way of saying that in order to be productive, the land must not be "raped" every day. Ecologically speaking, we say that Man, working or cultivating for his sustenance, must do so in full respect of the commandments of God; for example, he must cultivate for himself, for others by allowing the land to rest (Law of the Sabbath): The whole earth is at rest and quiet; they break forth into singing. the cypresses rejoice at you, the cedars of Lebanon, saying, 'Since you were laid low, no hewer comes up against us' (Is 14:7-8).

The law of uncultivated land (Ex 23:10-12; Deut 15:1-11; Lev 25:2-7, 18-22) gives its benefits to the poor but especially to the land in Lev 17:26, where the land itself must respect the resting of Yahweh, in the interests of its own time of renewal which is a right.

Hence if raped beyond measure, the land may revolt. This is what we find in Job 31:38-40 where the land "cries out" vengeance. This evocative text, decisive in this ecological era, says this: "If my land has cried out against me, and its furrows have wept together; if I have eaten its yield without payment, and caused the death of its owners; let thorns grow instead of wheat, and foul weeds instead of barley." Here the land is personified.

Pope Francis, the "green Pope"

For him, two major concerns should inspire the fight for life today, life as a gift from God who loves all his creatures: the land and the poor, intrinsically linked. These questions should be approached holistically, listening to "both the cry of the earth and the cry of the poor" (*Laudato Si'*, §49).

Dealing with various topics on pollution, waste, water, climate as a common good, the poor, Pope Francis says the quality of life today is deteriorating. And Man is responsible for this because of his politics, his political and social systems. Without denying the place of technology and science, he asks man to be capable of seeing himself and seeing everything that he puts in place. For "What kind of world do we want to leave to those who come after us, to children who are now growing up?" (*Laudato Si'*, §160). So he should have a care for future generations.

Supporter of integral ecology, lever of an integral human development, the Pope deals one after the other with environmental ecology, economic ecology, social ecology, cultural ecology and the ecology of everyday life, in this world stained with "consumerism and waste materials" (LS 109).

Bartholomé Ier, the "green Patriarch"

Going back to the declaration of Genesis 1:31, "CIT", the Orthodox Patriarch says that in fact the Greek word for "good" refers to beauty and not just goodness. So it is understood that the world was created beautiful. Having received creation in its physical, material dimension as a gift of grace, a gift accompanied by the commandment to serve and preserve the land, Adam and Eve (which is to say humanity) misused the gift of liberty, preferring to be detached from God the giver in order to attach themselves to God's gift"[12]. This is how original sin is to be understood. And still today in fact according to the Patriarch, all the pollution that spoils the face of the planet that was created beautiful, is an offence to the Creator.

Men and women are invited to be "eucharistic and ascetic" beings. The eucharistic dimension (*eucharisitia*, thanks, thanking) of man drives him to consider the whole of creation not as a possession nor as personal property, but as gift, present, a present touched with beauty, treasure of God the Creator. And if eucharistic Man uses natural resources, he will do so in a spirit of recognition.

The ascetic dimension of man (ascetic from *askéo*, treat a raw material through training and talent) leads to an ascetic ethos. Man the exploiter should willingly practise self-limitation and self-control, in the name of the love he has for humanity and for the whole of creation

---

[12] BARTHOLOMEE, ecumenical Patriarch, *Et Dieu vit que cela était bon*, Paris, Cerf, 2015, p. 20.

III. OF AN ETHICS AND A SPIRITUALITY OF CREATION

AN ECOLOGY FOR THE POOR

We want to take the example of the exploitation of a natural resource, notably forests which are a shared good in our African countries where their exploitation is either natural (for the indigenous peoples) or requires a permit for exploitation from the State (State Contract). But this does not exclude other natural resources. The forests we are speaking of are those in Mambéré Kadéi, west of the Central African Republic and east of Cameroon. But this is also true for other natural resources such as petrol, coltan, diamonds and gold, etc.

People's rights, ecological conscience and environmental justice

If the common good is to be fulfilled, there must be respect for the basic, inalienable rights of the human person. Education and health are the basic human rights. And in the sense of compensation, we ought to think of giving these peoples all the possibilities for satisfying these rights. No one should die for want of knowledge or for want of care. That would be a crime against humanity[13]. All those societies that are open to the felling of woods and forests, and also the State that authorises it, have social responsibilities towards those who live in these areas of exploitation of forests. Health insurance and the building of health centres that meet the consequent needs efficaciously are neither to be negotiated nor to be neglected. The lack of the most elementary medical care in those areas where the

---

[13] We know that the destruction of green space or of forests leads to an imbalance at the level of the ecosystem, which necessarily has effects on the natural environment. There are climatic and environmental problems, social and environmental risks. Life is disrupted and at the same time health is threatened.

ecological disaster is known to be making these areas of the planet hostile to Man and inhospitable is disrespect of Man, disrespect of his basic rights[14]. The Church must appeal to the responsibility of all decision-makers so that the lives of the peoples are respected. The Dominicans must speak out against this. In addition to the increased lack of infrastructures of training or instruction, the children of employees or among those peoples in areas of exploitation of forests do not have the benefit of adequate schooling. Now schooling, education, is for the acquisition of cultural and professional values. They have a right to "a human, civil culture"[15]. In no case must these youngsters be sacrificed – they are those who will be responsible tomorrow. Above all since already fathers of families spend the day in the fields and camps where trees are felled and sawed up.

There is water, too: access to drinkable water is a real problem[16]. We know that the right to water is a universal, hence inalienable right. All public organisms have a duty to give it to everyone. In fact, "The right to water... finds its basis in human dignity and not in any kind of merely quantitative assessment that considers water as a merely economic good. Without water, life is threatened"[17] The supplying of water, above all of drinkable water, is a matter of solidarity and respect for the dignity of the human person who has a right to life, and to healthy life. We may also say that ecological responsibility must drive Man to direct his activities in such a way as not to pollute natural water found in the forests, or rather in nature. For Benedict XVI, "CIT Message for world day of peace 2010)[18].

---

[14]Cf. John Paul II, Apostolic Letter *Novo millenium ineunte*, 50-51: AASS 93 (2001), 303-304.

[15] Pontifical 'Justice and Peace' Council, op. cit. n°557.

[16] On the fringe of the Forum on water held in Marseille, France from 12 to 17 March 2012, Luc MOCHAN, President of the World Council for Water, stated on the radio station RFI that according to the UNO, drinkable water is a fundamental right. For the expert, water purification is a poor relation in Africa; this results in a centre of sicknesses, a source of significant mortality.

[17] Compendium of the Social Doctrine of the Church n° 485.

[18] Benedict XVI

The problem of accommodation is part of the question of respect for human dignity.

I could not fail either to speak of the appropriation of lands for the "great" in our political régimes to the detriment of the populations that inhabit them: they are on vast territories that have already been purchased, waiting to be expelled, for those who blow hot and cold… This is the case in Cameroon.

For A Durable Développent

Durable development is "development that answers the needs of the present without compromising the ability of future generations to answer their own"[19]. In durable development there are two types of durability: spatial durability and temporal durability. Durable development is this development that has three dimensions: the economic, the social or societal and the ecological. Durable development is this economically viable, socially equitable and ecologically tolerable development. Each dimension has a specific purpose. In English this type of development is called "sustainable development". There are two important concepts in this definition of durable development: the needs of those who should have priority and the idea of limitation of the resources of the environment. In fact, Nature as environment is not inexhaustible; its capacity is limited and relative.

This is why we must promote an ecological conscience and establish an ecological justice.

This permits makes life possible today and tomorrow. The men and women of today and of tomorrow must live and enjoy the good things of the earth to the same degree, because they are all equal in dignity.

---

[19] Second Ecumenical Vatican Council, Pastoral Constitution *Gaudium et Spes*, 68: AAS 58 (1966), 1088-1089.

Universal destination of the goods of the earth and intergenerational equity

The management of the collective patrimony or common good demands that all be taken into consideration in equality. For in accordance with creation, the goods of the earth are intended for everyone, for all humanity, no one excluded. This is the principle of the universal destination of the goods of the earth: God intended the earth with everything contained in it for the use of all human beings and peoples. Thus, under the leadership of justice and in the company of charity, created goods should be in abundance for all in like manner.CIT GS 69 This right is natural, original, we may say divine. All this is for human development, which is a right and not merely an aspiration. The earth is an inheritance common to all humanity. It is important to distinguish between *intra*generational solidarity and *inter*generational solidarity to explain the reason for durable development.

Intragenerational solidarity has to do with all those who, belonging to the same generation, which means all living beings, do their utmost to ensure that everyone enjoys the fruits of the earth. It is true that the State claims to pursue people's happiness, but unless the State brings them together, it will not fulfil its intention. So what is needed is a participative development. Responsible use leads to development for everyone, for the thriving of all. I feel it is important to stress that increasingly (as was recalled during the 21st World Summit on the Climate in Paris, France in December 2015 – COP 21), the cultural and historical dimension must be a part of the approach to durable development.

Intergenerational solidarity claims to be concerned not only with the present but also with the future. In fact, "We are the heirs of earlier generations, and we reap benefits from the efforts of our contemporaries; we are under obligation to all men. Therefore we cannot disregard the welfare of those who will come after us to increase the human family. The reality of human solidarity brings us not only benefits but also obligations"[20]. This means that the Earth is an inheritance received and to be given. We are neither the first nor the last to occupy the Earth and enjoy its fruits. The Earth must be fertilized for today and for tomorrow. As René Coste puts it so effectively: "Planet Earth belongs to the future generations as much as to us, as a birthright"[21]. We should not steal from our neighbours near or far, steal their land.

IV. THE SPIRITUALITY OF CREATION

FIGHTING ECOLOGICAL EVIL OR FIGHTING EVIL IN THE ECOLOGICAL ERA

The problems related to the ecological crisis ride roughshod over the dignity of the human individual.

The evil of suffering or of poverty strikes dread in the human, Christian heart. Faced with social and economic exclusion, with the poverty of some of our kind, present and future (close neighbours and distant neighbours), we must find solutions in order to halt and banish all suffering. Solutions lie in solidarity. As the liberation theologian Gustavo Gutierrez says: "Poverty is an evil, a scandalous situation, which in our time has grown to enormous proportions. To eliminate it is to grasp more firmly the opportunity to see God face

---

[20] Paul VI, Encyclical *Populorum progressio*, 17, AAS 59 (1967) 266. For Benedict XVI, it is a matter of urgency to implement this intergenerational solidarity, because we must not allow the negative consequences of use of natural resources to weigh on future generations. Cf his message for Peace, 1 January 2010. John Paul II spoke of "the *urgent moral need for a new solidarity*" (Message, 1 January 1990, §10) and Benedict XVI of "*global solidarity*" (Message, 1 January 2009, §8).

[21] "*la planète-terre appartient aux générations futures autant qu'à nous par droit de naissance*", René Coste, Dieu et l'écologie, p.138.

to face, in the union with other people"[22]. The fight against poverty, in the sense of liberation of the human being, gives health to Man. Fighting to preserve human life gives health. In this sense, we can relate to this beautiful text, the only one that speaks to us directly of the Last Judgment: Matthew 25: 31-46.

This text shows Christ Jesus not as Judge, but as criterion of judgment – he who is the Love of God for Humanity, he who takes on the flesh" of all the little ones to whom we do this or that. Each one will be judged by her/his own acts, inspired by Love – Jesus Christ – or not. For Christ, Man in saved and so goes to Heaven if s/he respects three kinds of rights: the right to food (I was hungry, I was thirsty), the right to Community or Society (I was a stranger, I was naked) and the right to liberty (I was sick, I was in prison). All these rights of others, of present and/or future otherness can be applied to the duties of present-day technological Man.

Christ who is hungry or thirsty is the poor person, the being most threatened by the ecological crisis. We know that the worldwide food crisis, the lack of nourishment and of drinkable water, is the result of climate imbalance and climate change. Man is not innocent of the occurrence of this sad reality. Christ will tell us that we have made him suffer hunger and thirst.

Christ the stranger is every poor person who is excluded from the land of the living on the economic and social level. And yet everyone has a right to the good things of the earth. This is where we say that we must move from the principle of the universal destination of the goods of the earth. Furthermore, Christ naked is every individual without protection, victim of unjust laws, who cannot legitimately enjoy all the resources with which the Earth abounds. Present-day Man makes people naked and strangers, and

---

[22] *"la pauvreté est un mal, un état scandaleux, qui en notre période a pris d'énormes proportions. L'éliminer, c'est d'apporter plus étroitement l'occasion de voir Dieu face à face, dans l'union avec d'autres personnes"*, Gustavo Gutierrez, *Une Théologie de la Libération, de l'Histoire, de la Politique, et du Salut*, Orbis Book, New York, 1973, p. 106.

will recognise this before Christ.

Finally, as regards prisoners and the sick, we say that there are people who are victims of our senseless actions, actions of pollution that Pope Francis describes I this "culture of waste". Anyone who pollutes in various ways kills, because s/he causes illness and condemns others to a life of unhealthy precariousness. Our brothers and sisters in humanity may become prisoners of a life without attention to cleaning for a healthy, salutary environment, prisoners of a polluted life in polluted societies. Before we think only of large-scale industrial pollution, let's be sure: what do we do with our own waste? How do we manage it? Everything begins at our own door, let's think of our homes where all the management of waste materials starts with pre-collection, including selective sorting and the fact of continuing by means of the collection for the next stage of this sustainable management of the waste we produce every day. The environment influences human health in various ways. Man lives in the environment, carries out certain activities and these activities may have an impact on Man's own health. The Christ of the end of time, the Last Judgment, invites us to take on a human behaviour such that we may avoid an offence against human life. For human health owes its condition to the condition of the environment in which man lives, the condition of the environment that man develops.

"Another new" Christian ecological charter

Spirituality is a path, it will invite us on to a path, a path conducted in the Spirit. With Pope Francis who speaks of an ecological conversion, and Patriarch Bartholomé Ier who speaks of this same conversion of men and women into Eucharistic and ascetic beings, for René Coste the spirituality of creation must lead a new lifestyle, which must be less harmful for the environment. René Coste says that "our behaviour must be consistent with our collective struggle"[23].

To speak of the new relationship that Man must have with other creatures, René Coste goes back to an evocative thought that is at one and the same time ethical and spiritual[24]. This is a kind of prolonging of the Decalogue which we have in the Bible. In this Decalogue there are two tables: the first regards the relationship of Man to God and the second, the relationship of Man with his neighbour. The third table here regards the relationship of man with other creatures.

There are six new commandments that regard the management of the planet Earth. You shall not squander", "You shall seek quality of life", "You shall be indebted to to others for the goods of the planet", "You shall be responsible for your fertility", "You shall be responsible for your trash" and "You shall be responsible for the safeguarding of living species"[25]. It is in respecting all these commandments that Man assumes and ensures his responsibility towards other men and women, and towards the whole planet where he lives and for whose management he is responsible in the partnership with God.

We are all Dominicans, hence Christians, and we are on the road to eternal Life. These today are the challenges to our faith, our commitments. We will not be able to ignore this struggle out of respect for life on earth on the Road to the Other World.

We may say, then, that in our towns, we must promote purification: treat used waters, otherwise there will be harmful consequences on aquatic, animal, plant biodiversity, on human health. We may say, then, that in the sense of this management of our one and only planet, our towns and villages must all be "eco", they must become green towns, green villages. This means the birth

---

[23] Ibid., p.240.

[24] Here the author returns to the ideas developed in *Agir d'une manière responsable*, in *Fêtes et saisons, écologie et création*, April 1993, pp. 20-27.

[25] René Coste, op. cit., p. 244.

of eco-neighbourhoods, eco-villages, eco-towns. So we must make gardens, plant trees, revise our transport policy. Model towns are to be encouraged and imitated: true green towns like Kigali in Rwanda, where there are rubbish bins everywhere, service d'entretien soutenu. Hygiene and cleanliness services are à travailler. Community work is developed and encouraged. Everyone shpuld become aware of the importance of small gestures like the use of rubbish bins, du tri sélectif déjà dans nos ménages. In addition, the treatment of waters used by companies in our contrées. All this is with a view to the quality of life for humanity. For in polluting, we are killing today and tomorrow. We must also encourage the use of renewable energies with the geothermy, hydroelectricity etc. of their own energies.

As to the safeguarding of other species, we can only deplore the disappearance of certain species for which Man is to blame. Will we become aware of the importance of the food chain? When we say that the life of Man is linked to the life of Nature, we simply want to recall here the various functions of creatures: nourishing, reproductive, curative, protecting.

So we may think with Teihard de Chardin: "See, in the new space, a third way is emerging: to go to Heaven by way of the Earth"[26]. For a responsible relationship with the Earth expresses a good relationship with God and with humanity.

CONCLUSION

The Japanese philosopher Kazuoko Okadura had made it so clear: "Our god is great. Money is his prophet. For his sacrifices, we devastate all of Nature". Who is our God? Is he the one of whom the Japanese philosopher is speaking? We are often agents or accomplices in this devastation, this pollution of creation, for our

---

[26] Quoted on the inside back cover of René Coste, op. cit.

souls too are polluted. We must become aware that everything is linked today: the protection of nature, a truly human life for all, a new way of life. A revision and revisitation of the relationship between Man and the environment are urgent. For us Dominicans, knowing that justice and peace are an integral part of our preaching, the question of creation, of poverty, of development and of care of creation must be an integral part of our daily struggles in God, according to God. We must not strip ourselves of this.

Man, called to live his liberty in God, as a being blessed with reason, intelligence, will, is called to happiness without end with his Creator. Man, *Imago Dei*, must therefore do good deeds to be like God: to have eternal life. Good responsible deeds regarding the earth and towards/for its present and future inhabitants open up to this eternal Life. Any Christian answer or any human answer to the question "What have you done with your brother?" considered afresh makes this happiness possible. Techno-scientific, de-Christianized, secularized Man must recognize his responsibility in the current ecological crisis. So we must move from an arrogant fully alive anthropocentrism to a fully alive Christian anthropocentrism. Let us pray and act. May St Dominic our Father help us!

!

A Dominican View of Integral Human Development: The Agenda for the Laity

Duncan MacLaren, op

1. Introduction

Thank you for the invitation to the Congress. I must admit from the beginning that the group of Lay Dominicans which I belong to and which I co-founded over thirty years ago, is not a fraternity but is placed directly under the Master of the Order. Bro. Bruno mentioned the specialized lay Dominican groups in his address. The co-founders of our group were relatively young people then who wanted to come together as a group which expressed the charism of the Order as lived by laypeople, but also with an emphasis on justice and peace. We also thought that, as lay people, our lives could change rapidly and we might have to devote ourselves to babies, elderly parents or anything else life could throw at us. That discernment led us to decide to renew our commitment every three years rather than for life. That has enabled us to be active members while in the group because, for us, what was most important was the solid commitment to prayer, study, discernment and action to "transform the world" - or at least a little bit of it

THE PROBLEM

Let me start with what I regard as the problem of indifference or even animosity towards justice and peace as a concept within the Order. As a member of the International Dominican Justice and Peace Commission, I represent the laity with my colleagues, Teresita and Dimitri from Argentina and Guatemala respectively, with Dimitri representing the IDYM. At my first meeting in 2015, I was surprised at the reports from the friars and sisters in Europe, North America and Australasia - that they had difficulties finding promoters and that many young friars and sisters thought justice and peace old fashioned and dismissed the concept as a fad of the Sixties and Seventies. It was different in Africa, parts of Asia and Latin America. My fear is that it may be the same for the laity. Trying to elicit information about justice and peace activities from Lay Fraternities has proven very difficult for my contacts throughout the world and for me, partly because there is no reliable database of the lay groups involved in justice and peace and maybe partly because it seems too political - or old fashioned. I am grateful to those who did reply but, with some activities, I wonder where the justice element is.

The Catechism states, "Charity [by which is meant 'love'] is the greatest social commandment. It respects others and their rights. It requires the practice of justice, and it alone makes us capable of it".[1] Note that the word 'charity' is linked inextricably with justice in the teaching, not with being nice, kind or pious, even generous, but being just. And the Church, through Catholic Social Teaching, offers

---

[1] *Catechism of the Catholic Church* (1994) (London: Geoffrey Chapman, 1994) par. 1889.

a system which "proposes principles for reflection; it provides criteria for judgment; it gives guidelines for action", summed up in the Cardijn dialectic as 'see, judge, act'.[2] They are guidelines for action, not dogma as theory. You can't be dogmatic about the pains of the world. So, in terms of justice and peace, the Church has very clearly indicated what our mission should be – to transform the world by promoting justice and to save it by promoting peace.

In this presentation, I want to make four points. The *first* is how justice and peace thought and action is central to the Gospel and the lay Dominican charism of preaching it. The *second* is to suggest what this implies in general terms for Lay Dominicans domestically. The *third* is to explain the new term "Integral Human Development" since Pope Francis changed the Pontifical Council for Justice and Peace into the Dicastery for Promoting Integral Human Development. What is it and what does Pope Francis call us lay people to do? The *fourth* is to suggest some practical initiatives we can undertake to be more effective in the call to act on issues of integral human development. Bro. Bruno in his letter to the Congress reminds Lay Dominicans what their mission is in the words of *Lumen Gentium* – to be "sharers in their own way in the priestly, prophetic and kingly office of Christ…and [who] play their part in carrying out the mission of whole Christian people in the church and the world".[3]

I, however, don't want you to be passive listeners for an hour but active participants. I would like you to talk to your neighbours after the presentation and give us your opinion about the points made and the justice and peace actions which you feel your fraternity should undertake domestically and internationally.

---

[2] Ibid. par. 2423.

[3] Dogmatic Constitution of the Church (*Lumen Gentium*) in Austin Flannery OP, *Vatican Council II: The Basic Sixteen Documents,* Dublin: Dominican Publications, 1996) 1-95, par. 31.

2. POINT ONE: JUSTICE AND PEACE IS CENTRAL TO THE GOSPEL AND THE DOMINICAN CHARISM TO PREACH IT

Let's start by reminding ourselves of the three central tenets of the Catholic faith, that is, the principles which we, as Catholic Christians, hold are true:-

Kerygma – (a Greek word meaning 'proclamation' - Word) preaching the word of God, not just in Sunday homilies or sermons but with our lives. The great Flemish Dominican theologian, Edward Schillebeeckx OP, said we write a fifth Gospel with our lives. We preach a faith based on the Reign of God which begins here on Earth among the messiness of our lives and our societies, national and international. That means preaching on the homeless on our streets; pointing out that when hurricanes take lives, they take more in so-called developing countries than they do in the so-called developed whose lifestyle caused the increase in crazy weather in the first place; denouncing economic experiments such as structural adjustment programmes in the past which may help bankers in the West but cost lives and misery in the poorest nations. As Dominicans, we are called to denounce what is wrong with the world; we are called to action which takes the sides of the poorest; and in that way we witness to the life, death and resurrection of Jesus.

Leitourgia – (Greek for 'public service' - Worship) worship and it's obviously where we derive our term 'liturgy' from. Worship is important. The sacraments and prayer take us beyond ourselves so that we can love others, not just ourselves. Timothy Radcliffe, the former Master of the Order, wrote "I discover what love is when I let her be the centre of the world and not myself".[4] When we are no longer the centre of our world but other people *are*, then we 'put on', as St Dominic said, not just truth but the mantle of solidarity. Solidarity isn't, as Saint John Paul II wrote, "a feeling of vague compassion or shallow distress at the misfortunes of so many

---

[4] Timothy Radcliffe OP, *I Call You Friends*, (London: Continuum, 2001) 50.

people". No, "it is a firm and persevering determination to commit oneself to the common good; that is to say to the good of all and of each individual, because we are all really responsible for all".[5] The common good has been characterised by our South African brother, Albert Nolan OP, as "whatever is best for the whole human family, or the whole community of living beings or the whole universe in its grand unfolding".[6]

And the last tenet of our faith is *diakonia*,

Diakonia – (Greek word for ministering - World) the ministry of serving society, human dignity and human rights. Ministering to the world is not on the margins of the faith (as often can seem the case) but central and this is where justice and peace as a concept prefiguring the Reign of God is brought together, not just as 'projects' but as a life choice. As Pope Francis says in *Evangelii Gaudium* (The Joy of the Gospel), quoting the Latin American bishops, "the mission of proclaiming the Good News of Jesus Christ has a universal destination. Its mandate of charity encompasses all dimensions of existence, all individuals, all areas of community life, and all peoples. Nothing human can be alien to it".[7] Equally, *Gaudium et Spes* taught us to be more positive towards the world where the laity above all have to read the signs of the times and act to transform the world.

Though *diakonia* specifically has a focus on building a just society, the other two central tenets, as I have tried to illustrate, are also radically social because the Gospel is radically social. It is permeated with stories about transforming ourselves to serve others and transforming our society to be more just.

As for the Order, if we ask whether Dominic was a justice and peace activist from the beginning of his mission, the answer is

---

[5] Pope John Paul II, *Sollicitudo Rei Socialis*, (Vatican City: Libreria Editrice Vaticana, 1987), par. 38.

[6] Albert Nolan OP, *Jesus Today: A Spirituality of Radical Freedom*, (Maryknoll, NY: Orbis Books, 2006) 188.

[7] Pope Francis *Evangelii Gaudium*, (London: CTS, 2013), par.181.

probably 'no'. He preached God's mercy towards sinners, calling them back to the Catholic faith. But St Dominic, as the Glasgow Lay Dominican constitution states, was also so moved by the terrible poverty he saw around him that he sold his beloved books to feed the people, saying "I could not bear to prize dead skins when living skins were starving and in want". And it is St Thomas Aquinas who tells us to embrace justice and peace as legitimate Dominican issues in his discussion of justice in the *Summa* as being "a particular virtue disposing us to give others their due as God's creatures and our neighbours".[8]

To conclude on this point about the centrality of justice and peace to our faith and our charism as Dominicans, it is clear that justice and peace is not just part of *diakonia* but is central to *kerygma* and *leitourgia* also yet it is so often sidelined in parish life. You know the situation - the *real* Catholics attend the prayer groups while the others form justice and peace groups, and there is little dialogue between the two. We need to go on a rosary procession as we did the other night here in Fatima to pray for ourselves, the Church and the world – and go on a march for peace in the world. We need to do both, as Pope Emeritus Benedict XVI indicates in Caritas in Veritate. For our faith to be lived authentically, we need all three tenets of the faith to come together in an integrated whole in our lives, as individuals and as members of Dominican fraternities and other lay groups, and in our living out of our faith in the world.

Let me turn to point two.

3. POINT TWO: IF JUSTICE AND PEACE IS CENTRAL TO THE PREACHING OF THE GOSPEL, HOW SHOULD LAY DOMINICANS ACT IN A DOMESTIC CONTEXT?

Let me give you my take on this question. First, we have to be

---

[8] From Richard Finn OP, "Early Voices for Justice" in John Orme Mills OP 3.(ed.), *Justice, Peace and Dominicans 1216-2001,* (Dublin: Dominican Publications, 2001) 19-30, 23.

most concerned about the world where people made in the divine image live, especially the most marginalised. The injustices they suffer constitute the agenda which the mission of the Church calls us to transform. Solidarity demands that we look at the injustice through the eyes of those suffering the injustice. As Timothy Radcliffe said in his letter to the Order, 'Vowed to Mission' (1994), "you get a different view of the world depending if you're looking at it from the seat of a Mercedes or the seat of a bicycle"[9] so we have to take the option for the poor seriously.

For that reason, I would suggest that the modern manifestation of St Dominic's selling his books to feed people is to work to change the economic, social and political structures that cause such poverty and marginalisation in the first place. Today's Good Samaritan is a political lobbyist for justice.

Various General Chapters of the Order have indicated what preaching justice should look like. Oakland said that actions for justice and peace must meet three criteria:- they must be communal, specifically integrated into local, provincial and regional projects; they must be well thought out and based on a serious analysis of the social reality and be rooted in strong Biblical and theological foundations; they must ensure the support of brothers, sisters and the laity to participate actively - even to the point of risking their lives - in associations and movements for the promotion of human dignity.

Bro. Bruno in his letter to this Congress[10] mentions groups of people and areas which should be at the centre of our concern as

---

[9] Timothy Radcliffe OP, "Vowed to Mission" in (no editor) *To Praise, to Bless, to Preach: Words of Grace and Truth,* (Dominican Publications: Dublin, 2004) 327-347, 342.

[10] Bruno Cadoré OP, Le*tter to the Laity of the Order of Preachers,* 25th January 2018. Retrieved from http://archive.fraternitiesop.com/810_17_73_ICLDF_English_01.25.18 .pdf.

Lay Dominicans in link with the Order as a whole. He mentions, first, refugees, asylum seekers, migrants and stateless people, human beings among the 66 million forced to leave their homes, countries and citizenship through war, conflict, dehumanising poverty or oppression. The Master of the Order talks about families, interestingly, particularly those which are dysfunctional, rather than the rather romantic view held by the official Catholic imagination. Allied to that, he mentions how we should be active in welcoming and integrating those in so-called "irregular" relationships since, as Pope Francis says, "No-one can be condemned for ever because that is not the logic of the Gospel".[11] Bro. Bruno mentions human rights in all its forms as a site for our action and compassion and we have the reports of the Congress in Salamanca of 2016 as outstanding resources for us. Lastly, the Master mentions participation in interreligious dialogue and ecumenism with our fellow Christians, both in terms of understanding one another and working together with them on all the other issues.

We also have a distinct, Gospel-based methodology - an extension of 'see, judge, act' called the pastoral spiral. We should first observe the injustice through experience and human encounter; second, we should analyse the causes and consequences of the injustice to the dignity of human lives; third, we should theologically reflect on the result of this analysis to discern our response in the light of the Gospel and Church social teaching; and, finally, we must act based on the first three steps to plan, set goals, determine strategies and share tasks; and then, before beginning again with a new subject, evaluate what we have done.

Let me give two examples of what this methodology can lead to. When I met members of a Lay Fraternity in a town in Cameroun, they told me that through their discernment to assist the poorest,

---

[11] Pope Francis, *Amoris Laetitia (The Joy of Love)*, (London: Catholic Truth Society, 2016) par. 297.

they decided to focus on that part of their population living with HIV/AIDs, and found themselves not only accompanying the people, but also in trying to persuade the community to get rid of the stigma and embrace their suffering brothers and sisters. This, too, is a modern instance of St Dominic's selling his books for the poor except for our Cameroonian brothers and sisters what they are giving is their time and loving presence, resulting in increased self-esteem for the most marginalised Other.

In my own city of Glasgow, the Lay Dominicans discerned that we should work with young drug addicts from our deprived areas. We stayed overnight with youngsters at a house halfway between the prison they had just left and the professional drug rehabilitation centre they were going to. Our task was to be welcoming, make them at ease and listen to them talk about their experiences – chat which often went on till dawn. We Dominicans brought our concern, loving presence and listening skills as well as humour to kids some of whom felt they had ruined their lives at 17 years old.

In both examples, we agreed that, in the way of the Gospel, the poor changed us, took us to the depths of our compassion and strengthened our commitment to the preferential option for the poor, and to advocate to change the perception of people towards those living with HIV and AIDs and drug users in two very different scenarios. In Bruno's list or in your own social analysis of your town, village or area, you'll be able to discern what you can do as Dominicans to bring justice and the love of Christ to others. Remember the Congress on Human Rights in Salamanca in 2016 where we committed ourselves to "embrace as an integral part of our Dominican charism, the mission of justice and peace as constitutive to the preaching of the Gospel".[12] Let us as Lay Dominicans strengthen that commitment at this Congress.

---

[12] Final Statement of the Salamanca Congress on Human Rights, 2016. Retrieved from http://www.op.org/en/content/final-statement-salamanca-congress-human-right-2016.

4. POINT THREE: FROM JUSTICE AND PEACE TO INTEGRAL HUMAN DEVELOPMENT

Pope Francis is adept at, as we say in colloquial English, "throwing a spanner in the works", that is, changing our perspectives about matters to draw us further into the heart of the Gospel and away from our complacencies about the faith. When he announced he was not only changing the name of the Pontifical Council for Justice and Peace in the Vatican but putting the dicasteries (the Vatican equivalent of ministries in a Government) for charitable works, health, migration and the care of creation into the new Dicastery for Promoting Integral Human Development, there was a sharp intake of breath in the corridors of the Curia. What was coming now from this prophetic Pope?

Maybe he changed the name of the dicastery because he thought the phrase 'justice and peace' had run its course. Maybe he thought that the new name, with its origins in Blessed Pope Paul VI's 1967 encyclical on development, *Populorum Progressio* ("The Progress of Peoples"), emphasised the human at the centre of a development which had to cover not just economics but all life, including the transcendent; that it had to be understood in the light of the Gospel; and had to be aimed at maintaining the dignity of the human person in all circumstances.

I suspect he also thought that 'justice and peace' had become a process whereby the poor were becoming the object of someone else's idea of how they should be developed rather than that they should be the subjects of their own development, incorporating their cultural and religious values and allowing them to be, the agents of their own destiny.

In his address[13] at the fiftieth celebration of *Populorum Progressio*

---

[13] Pope Francis, "Address on the 50th Anniversary of the Encyclical *Populorum Progressio*", 4th April 2017. Retrieved from https://zenit.org/articles/popes-address-to-vatican-conference-on-50th-anniversary-of-populorum-progressio/.

in April 2017, Pope Francis explained what he meant by integral human development: that this type of development is about integrating the peoples of the Earth by ensuring that the gap between the rich and the poor lessens; about offering practical models of social integration, ensuring no-one is excluded; about integrating the individual and communal dimensions, and shunning selfish individualism, as can be seen in parts of the Western world by the rise of the new right in politics which wants to bar distant strangers fleeing violence, oppression and poverty or which seeks to build walls between people rather than bringing them down; that this development model is about integrating body and soul, taking into account the transcendent aspect of people's lives, and integrating Catholic Social Teaching into our thoughts and actions on the social and political aspects of living in our present world. The term does not supplant 'justice and peace' but makes it, in my view, more concrete in our context and makes the faith element much more visible.

And so we come to our last point

5. POINT FOUR: ACTING AS LAY DOMINICANS ON INTEGRAL HUMAN DEVELOPMENT ISSUES BEYOND OUR SHORES

John Orme Mills OP has a chapter in *The Grace and Task of Preaching* in which he says that we should remind people that "our lives as Christians are bound up not only with our inner hopes, fears and temptations, and not only with the people around us but also with those huge global issues".[14] We must show how those big issues of integral human development, being an interdependent world, are intimately linked to the way we live, vote and build up society, and that we are co-responsible for the social sins that beset our planet.

---

[14] John Orme Mills OP, "Preaching on the Wider World" in Michael Monschau O.P. (ed.) *The Grace and Task of Preaching*, (Dublin: Dominican Publications, 2006) 314-328, 314-315.

We should not just relegate them to the prayers of the faithful.

These big issues can seem daunting. Under the leadership of Margaret Mayce OP at the UN in New York and Mike Deeb OP at the UN in Geneva, we have the information, agendas and networks which will enable us to tackle these issues at the international level as the Dominican family. The UN may not be perfect but it is the only international secular moral voice we have to act for justice and peace in our world. What they lack is hearing the voice of the poorest from the grassroots and that is what we can provide along with other congregations (as well as Caritas) who live and suffer with the poorest.

In Caritas, Archbishop Odama of Gulu in the north of Uganda pleaded with Caritas Uganda to tell the world about the brutal civil war where children were abducted, brutalised and forced by the ironically named Lord's Resistance Army to kill their families and friends. They contacted us in Caritas Internationalis in Rome and we alerted our delegate in the UN in New York and the Archbishop was invited to address the Security Council. Six months later, there was a fragile ceasefire because Archbishop Odama could talk of named people whose children had been taken from them and describe what happened to them. Not all politicians in the UN have hearts of stone, and even those who do might be persuaded by such witness to change their mind.

The Dominican Order is international, found at the grassroots and has active networks which can make the voices of those who have no voice heard all the louder so that a bit more justice may enter our world. All it takes from us is passion to start, passion to analyse and discern, and passion to act.

Let me give you two concrete possibilities for collective action. The Order has already adopted the month of December as the "Dominican Month for Peace", when we are urged to pray for peace in a designated part of the world, offer solidarity to a particular 'project' and highlight the plight of the people. Last year, it was

Colombia, and this year the focus will be the Democratic Republic of Congo (DRC) where the Church has been on the streets supporting the people in their thirst for democracy in a country which is rich and resources and has some of the worst poverty and appalling conflict in the world. Information will be sent out soon to the Order and it is beholden on us after this Congress to undertake whatever solidarity actions are asked of us to accompany and assist the suffering people of DRC.

The second possibility is that, just as in the past the Order launched a Dominican Family project for the Millennium Development Goals (MDGs), so it is likely the Commission will recommend to the Master and his advisors that all branches of the Order should work together to campaign on the MDGs' successor, the Sustainable Development Goals (SDGs). They are an agenda of seventeen universal goals to improve our world from 2016 to 2030, and are directed to all countries, not just the so-called 'developing' countries. The National Director of Caritas Kenya, Stephen Kituku, said of the Goals, that he hoped they would differ from the MDGs which were created through a top-down, closed-door process that did not engage people living in poverty. In other words, the very opposite of an integral human development approach. Stephen stated, "This is our generational chance to make it right".[15] It is a wonderful opportunity for the Dominican Family internally to cooperate together on a project that, if successful, will rid our world of dehumanising poverty, improve the situation of women and children especially, and bring climate change, as Pope Francis suggests in *Laudato Si'*, into the centre of our actions to save the planet.

Let me conclude. I started by pointing out our problem about justice and peace in the Order. Hopefully I have outlined how it is central to Church teaching as well as having been practice in the

---

[15] For details of what all the members of Caritas Internationalis are doing about the SDGs, see the website www.caritas.org.

Order since our beginnings. I have mentioned how I think we can act – and, indeed, have been acting for many centuries – to this Gospel call for action about saving our planet and ridding our world of dehumanising poverty; and how we have a distinct methodology for serving humanity and making sure our promises of positive change become true. I have tried to express why Pope Francis now prefers the term 'Integral Human Development' in which justice and peace find their place by narrowing the gap between the rich and the poor, the included and the excluded; by putting community before individualism as seen in the principle of the common good; by integrating body and soul by ensuring that all belief systems and culture find their central place in any development process; where the poor and marginalised are empowered and participate in deciding how they and their community should spearhead their own idea of what 'being developed' means as opposed to the western model so tainted by neo-liberal capitalism; and that we can all learn from the example of the empowered poor. I ended with two examples of how we can work together with the other branches of the Order as the Dominican Family on the UN Sustainable Development Goals and the Dominican month for peace in DRC.

As we all sadly know, our Church has, in the past decade, lost a great deal of credibility through the sexual scandals which continue to blight us. We are in crisis but a crisis presents us also with an opportunity. An opportunity to put the integration of our intellect, spirituality and praxis to work for humanity. We can no longer say that we are perfect – but we never were; we can no longer claim to be saints – but only very few of us were. We can claim, however, to listen, to contemplate and to share the actions arising out of our contemplation with those in, as the soon-to-be Blessed Pierre Laverie OP said, the 'fractures' of a broken world. That is what being involved in integral human development means, and that is the truth that we can bring. As our sister, St Catherine of Siena, said, "Preach the Truth as if you have a million voices. It is silence that kills the world". Let us, in the tradition of our Order, raise our voices for peace and justice in Cameroon, Venezuela, the Dominican Republic and anywhere else where humanity suffers at the hands of evil. In the Congress, we have talked a lot about faith *in* Christ but let us now also follow the faith *of* Christ, and bring mercy and compassion to others and help transform our world to be just so that everyone, but especially the poorest, may flourish.

Thank you.

CHRIST IS OUR PEACE (EF 2, 17)
Fr. Gerald Stookey, op

1. WE BELIEVE IN JESUS CHRIST

After a ten-year moratorium on executions in the United States, the U.S. Supreme Court reinstated the death penalty in 1976, amid a diversity of protest campaigns. I was on the staff of the Justice and Peace Commission of the Archdiocese of Denver, Colorado, and participated in a state-wide coalition effort to prevent possible enactment on this new ruling.

At an initial planning meeting, representatives from political, civic and religious organizations each presented themselves and the reasons they were opposed to the death penalty. The rationale for opposition was justifiably long. For example: overwhelming racism in the arrests and incarceration of criminals; higher sentencing of the poor class who could not pay for proper legal defense; and the danger of executing innocent victims who received unfair trials.

When it came time for the Catholic Archdiocese to present its participation in the coalition, my boss, Auxiliary Bishop George Evans, stated: "We agree with most of the arguments that the rest of you have presented against the death penalty, and certainly we can work in coalition with you. However, our Catholic reasons go even further. We are not in favor of capital punishment under any circumstances, *even if* you can end discrimination in the police department and the court system. We are not in favor of the death penalty *even if* poor and rich get equal treatment under the law. And *even if* we could guarantee that the criminal to be executed is absolutely guilty, we would still be opposed to capital punishment. For we believe that every person is created in the *image of God*, even criminals, and that only God has the right to give and take life. With true compassion for the victims of crime, we believe in the forgiveness and love of Jesus Christ, even for criminals."

His statement created a loud silence over the group. Even so, a year later, we lost our campaign to stop the death penalty when Gary Mark Gilmore became the first to be executed on January 17, 1977. That day Bishop Evans arrived at our office in tears to report the sad news. Since then, at the time of this writing, the United States has executed 1,483 prisoners, with 2,743 prisoners presently on what is called "death row". Nevertheless, I have never forgotten the profound impact that Bishop Evans' words had on everyone in our campaign, primarily because of the clarity of the Christian position, as he stated it to us.

2. THE IMPORTANCE OF ASKING WHY?

Bishop Evans' words inspired all of us on the Archdiocesan Justice & Peace Commission to keep before us always *WHY* we work for justice and peace. It is an important question for all of us at this Congress dedicated to the them of Justice & Peace & the Care of Creation. Do we know why we are doing this? Do those of us who are committed to justice and peace and the care of creation keep before us the core mission and the purpose behind all our efforts. Perhaps much opposition to justice and peace is due to lack of clarity of purpose on our part.

Many of have read Viktor Frankl's *Man's Search For Meaning* (1946), which I read during my university days, describing how he survived the Nazi concentration camp because "those who have a 'why' to live, can bear with almost any 'how' ." If we know why we are Dominicans and why we are for justice and peace, then we will be able to put up with any oppposition.

Translated into many languages, Lewis Carroll's *Alice in Wonderland* (1865) is one of the world's favorite fairy-tales. Do you recall where the Cheshire Cat wisely advises Alice that "If you don't know where you are going, then any road will get you there"? If we are going to spend a lot of time, effort and money working for justice and peace, we better know where we want to go.

In his book *Start With Why: how great leaders inspire everyone to take action* (2009), Simon Sinek warns: "When a WHY goes fuzzy, it becomes much more difficult to maintain the growth, loyalty and inspiration that helped drive the original success". Jesus and Dominic knew their Why and their "original success" over 2000 and 800 years ago continue to inspire us and many others, so long as we don't let it "go fuzzy".

Sadly, many individuals in the world have no idea what they are doing or where they are going. They live an "unexamined life", as Socrates would say. Some lack hope and are suicidal because they have no **Why**, no meaning, just going down any road of fuzzy existence. On the other hand, we encounter others who know exactly what they want and where they want to go, but whose **Why** is in direct opposition to ours. They can easily "out-organize" fuzzy thinkers and clueless actors. So, although it may seem elemental and pedantic, it behooves all Dominicans, especially at this International Congress, to reflect again and articulate plainly our **Why**, our initial call. Then we will inspire others to act with us, hopefully because of the greater clarity of our proposition. Don't agonize; organize—and know the Why behind what we are and do.

3. OUR WHY:

Of course, Jesus and Dominic, you and I, we all find our first and foremost *Why* to be God. Like the *Creed*, we begin with "I believe in God..." Great minds try to articulate faith in God in a rational way, but it almost always falls short of words, which makes explaining our primary *Why* to opponents very challenging.

St. Thomas Aquinas writes in his *Summa Theologica* (I q.9a,1) that "there is some First reason called God". St. Anselm says that God is "that than which nothing greater can be thought." For many of us, the very existence of anything brings us to faith in God. Playing on Descartes, "If I exist, therefore God exists"--for who of us knows how to create a universe? The greatest good, perfect love, the most merciful and compassionate, wisest and spiritual being, this is what we mean by God and who gives us believers our starting *Why*.

Of course, not everybody believes in God, as we know. In fact, it seems the battle about the existence of God has never raged so strongly as in our modern times. There is no end to Karl Marx, Sigmund Freud, Andrew Flew, Carl Sagan, Christopher Hitchens, Stephen Hawking and the long litany of modern atheists, agnostics, and secular and scientific humanists. They are organized and demand that we state *WHY* we believe in God and also *WHY* we are working for justice and peace and the care of creation. If you haven't met them yet, you soon will!

We believe, as Aquinas says, that there is something supreme, something spiritual, something perfect that is NOT material, greater than mathematics, greater than human reason or consciousness. God is the meaning and center of our life, our first and foremost *Why* to everything.

If we do not personally have God as our primary *WHY* as Dominicans for justice and peace, we will "go off the rails", take any road to who knows where, and end up misunderstood, and rightfully accused of simply playing politics or fomenting social revolution. We will not inspire others if they do not understand "where we are coming from"--from our belief in God. Then we would fail to teach, as the Jesuits say, "the faith that does justice", or as Dominicans, we would neglect to clarify that we are "preaching the just Word".

So let's not be cowardly but rather let our *God-Why* be known and apparent to the world, and in a particular way to fellow, resistant Christians, and yes, even to resistant Dominicans, who accuse our ministry of justice and peace to be nothing more than faithless foolishness.

4. JESUS: "THE FATHER AND I ARE ONE" (JOHN 10:30).

For us Christians, the best example of God's existence is Jesus of Nazareth, God's only Son. God is not abstract. Jesus the Christ is God-with-us. As St. John writes "God so loved the world that he gave us his only begotten Son" (John 3:16).

I am a bit surprised at how little we Dominican preachers talk about Jesus if he is our primary *Why*. How can we preach One whom we do not know? Who do you say that Jesus is *for you personally?* I'm sure we don't all see Jesus the same. So let me offer some of my own reflections about Jesus, in light of His being our *WHY* for preaching justice and peace and caring for creation.

Jesus of Nazareth, being faithful to Torah and his Jewish tradition, referred to God as his "Father"--that's who he said that God is for him . He totally identified his life with God, saying "the Father and I are one" (John 10:30). Jesus believes His God as *Abba* is pure love, who loves and cares for us like a good Father. Jesus says that God showers us with good things and takes care of us, as he does the sparrows, and will never abandon us. Despite the bad times in which Jesus lived, he offers surprising hope and joy in his teaching, simply because of God's love for us. There's a kind of "invincible" belief in goodness in Jesus' teachings, reminding us constantly not to worry, not to be afraid, to be at peace, to forgive one another. For, God loves us, forgives us, treats us with compassion, and considers all of us to be God's children. Jesus' God has a particular concern for the oppressed, poor and down-trodden. His prophetic condemnation is primarily for those who are unjust, oppressors, abusers of their wealth and titles. Most of his Good News seems to be directed especially to "those at the bottom". For the rich, it's actually bad news.

The modern search for the "historical Jesus" is controversial as you can read in *The Historical Jesus: a comprehensive guide* by Gerd Theissen and Annette Merz (1996), and *What Are They Saying About the Historical Jesus* by David B. Gowler (2007). Some interpretations of Jesus in the past and still today are clearly erroneous and are proven to be nothing more than a "domesticated Jesus" to fit the time, culture, and biases of a particular preacher, Christian group, or hostile enemy of Christians. At times, what Jesus said and did are intrinsically left open to interpretation, like his parables, as noted in *The Parables After Jesus: their imaginative receptions across two millenia* by David B. Gowler (2017), which presents a fascinating array of how Jesus' parables were variably received throughout history, such as in art and music. That's how parables are! How do justice and peace advocates interpret Jesus' parables?

Apart from theological interpretations, as a sociologist I cannot ignore the "sociological" aspects about Jesus of Nazareth, that are interesting in light of our justice and peace ministry:

- he is Jewish and studied Jewish Scriptures;
- he is poor and he experienced extreme poverty all around him;
- he is from a minority group in Galilee, Palestine;
- he lived in the first century Mediterranean world;
- his country was occupied by the Roman Empire with its strong-armed soldiers and governors;
- he lived amidst a great deal of political and theocratic unrest and rivalries (Herodians, Essenes, Pharisees, etc.);
- he was known as the son of a carpenter;
- his parents were refugees to Egypt in order to save his life;

- his family included his mother who was named, Mary; his father who was named, Joseph; his relatives, Elizabeth and Zachary, and their son, John;
- possibly he was a disciple of John, and was baptized by him;
- he emerged as a prophetic, wandering, charismatic preacher at around 30 years old;
- he was known as a healer, teacher, rabbi, miracle-worker who associated with the poor, sinners, sick, outcast; hungry; excluded;
- he is a layman, not a priest from the Temple;
- he formed a "new school" of wandering disciples, with a core group of Twelve;
- a good number of his Twelve were originally fishermen, also economically poor;
- he and they walked a lot, up and down Palestine;
- he had no permanent home to call his own;
- he had close friends who cared for him like Mary Magdela, Mary & Martha, Lazarus.
- he repeatedly broke with Jewish tradition especially purity and sabbath laws;
- he broke with social custom on relating to women, foreigners, non-believers;
- enemies tried to kill him several times, and eventually succeeded;
- he was betrayed and "played off" between religious and political authorities;
- he was detained, tortured and executed by the Roman Empires' infamous death penalty: crucifixion.
- He died quite young at around 33 years old.

These human "biographical facts" of Jesus, apart from the fact of His Divine Resurrection, help us understand much of what he said and did, in light of justice and peace. Jesus' *personal identities* indicate that God sent him under these human conditions with a very specific message to the world. This Jesus from Nazareth, the Christ, is *THE WHY* we preach and act for justice, peace and creation.

5.   JESUS FOR JUSTICE:

Some years ago I taught at Regis University in Denver, Colorado USA, in the Peace and Justice Studies department. At the very beginning of the Introductory Course on Peace and Justice, I asked the students to list some of their favorite figures in history who they admire as heroic supporters of justice and peace. Of course, many agreed that Mahatma Gandhi was a great pacifist. Dr. Martin Luther King, Jr. was also at the top of their list as a non-violent defender of civil rights for African-Americans. Some included Abraham Lincoln, the American civil war president who opposed slavery. Dorothy Day, the foundress of the Catholic Worker Movement in my country was named over and over. Bartolomé de Las Casas, the Dominican defender of the American Indians was acknowledged. Some mentioned Catholic saints: Francis of Assisi, lover of creation and the poor and promoter of peace; Martin de Porres, patron of social justice; Mother Teresa of Calcutta, pro-life advocate of the unwanted and untouchables. Who are your favorite saints, heroes and heroines for justice throughout history? Well, the curious thing is: no students ever listed Jesus of Nazareth! Perhaps we Christians ourselves do not think Jesus is for justice and peace? We not only need to talk about who Jesus is for us, but what we mean by justice.

Very common among us is the perception that working for the poor, doing charity, helping others, is the same thing as working for justice. While they are definitely related, I think we can make some Dominicans distinctions between social services or charitable works and our efforts for social justice and non-violent change. St. Vincent de Paul Society, Catholic Charities, Catholic Relief Services, Red

Cross, Caritas International are essentially emergency relief and social outreach organizations to help the poor, although many of them include some effort to *advocate for* the poor too. They are very important in helping with victims of injustice, war, emergencies, natural disasters. All Christians should support them and I have rarely heard arguments against Christians doing charity. However, I would like us to consider a difference of Justice and Peace individuals and organizations that are essentially working to change unjust laws and social structures, getting at the causes of so many poor victims, defending human rights, social action, and advocacy to correct injustice. Dom Helder Camara of Brazil once said "When I give food to the poor they call me a saint; when I ask why they are poor they call me a communists". That why some don't like justice and peace--they simply don't like the questions we ask.

There is a famous story that is told to help us understand the distinction between Charity and Justice efforts:

Once two friends were walking along a river praying the rosary, when one of them noticed a baby drowning in the river. They both jump in and save the baby. Then they noticed another baby in the water, and then another. An emergency response team was set up, which eventually included an orphanage and pediatric field hospital. They got volunteers and donations of food and clothes for the poor babies. As this went on for some time, one of the them started to leave the emergency situation at the river. The other cried out "Hey, where are you going? Don't you see we have babies drowning in this river here?" The other friend replied "Yes, and we need to keep saving them. But now it is time for some of us to get together and go upstream and stop whoever is throwing them in and to stop them."

If I exaggerate this story in light of our Congress theme, I would say the first friend who stays at the river helping out charitably is a Franciscan. The one who goes upstream to study whoever is throwing the babies into the river, preaches against it, and act for justice for the babies is a Dominican. Dominicans, if anyone, should be the ones who preach justice. Even with this simplistic distinction between Charity and Justice, some Christians will never be for justice and peace, or going upstream to try and change things. They may fear it. It's scary.

Most definitions of social justice have to do with how society ought to provide access to materials and services in a fair way. Who gets what stuff, how much do they get, and who decides what they get, what structures and systems are needed to provide it? This is what is called **distributive justice**.

In some cases, it is simply an equal distribution of things like water, electricity or sanitation, or an equality in basic rights such as the right to life, to eat, to breathe, etc. **Equality in distributive justice** is found in Scripture, as we believe everyone is created equal in the eyes of God (imago Dei) and that God's grace falls equally on the just and the unjust, like rain or sunshine falling equally on the good and the bad alike. Jesus feeds 5000 hungry people equally, not asking the disciples to separate out the deserving or worthy poor from those who had eaten earlier or those who had money on them. He fed them all. In this miracle, Jesus distributes bread in a way that is **equal justice for all.**

The dilemma arises where our needs are not equal, and so we are called to provide **distributive justice based on needs**. "From each according to his ability, to each according to his/her need", as Karl Marx stated it, curiously borrowing from Acts 4:35. For example, those living in Lithuania need more heat and clothing than those in the Dominican Republic. Equal distribution would be unfair when we encounter such a *needs-based* situation. Jesus told the Parable of the Day Laborers who all got the same pay although they worked different hours? So it was not really the same pay but very "unequal" pay. Perhaps Jesus knew that the last to go to work has great need of a full day's salary too. The Prodigal Son had greater need of forgiveness and celebration upon his return, even though the older son had been more responsible throughout his life. So in another context, Jesus' sense of justice allows for those who have greater needs than others, and *in that need, not all are equal.*

The complaints of the hard workers and older sons is precisely what leads some to invent a **distributive justice system based on merit.** They say it is unfair if they have worked harder. This merit-based justice can be un-Christian and drives the heated debate about helping only the poor who are "worthy". The unworthy poor do not try hard enough to "pull themselves up by their own bootstraps". Jesus the carpenter's son, and his fishermen disciples, were all poor, who preached and acted as though all the poor were worthy. I do not see Jesus supporting such a merit-based distribution of justice that has to be earned.

The American philosopher, John Rawls, calls for "justice as fairness" in his writing *A Theory of Justice* (1971). He says we are certainly equal in our basic rights, but must support those who are disadvantaged, often beyond their control, like your place or status at birth. He says that the playing field is uneven from the start; some more privileged, others disadvantaged. I was born in the United States and had no trouble getting into Portugal, while many others in Bolivia or Philippines could not even get a visa to come! And don't forget that I am also an American who is a white, older male, with academic degrees, also a Catholic Dominican priest, all of which probably shows up somewhere in my file! If you recall the biographical data we mentioned regarding Jesus of Nazareth inside Palestine, he would not have gotten a visa to attend here either! I have unfair merits and privileges. So, there needs to be **fairness in distributive justice**.

Rawls developed what he called the "original position" or starting point for doing justice. That is, think about what kind of society we would like *if* you didn't know what your original position in that society would actually be. Try it on yourself: What sort of justice would you like to be "born into" *if* you didn't really know beforehand what your original position in society would be? Would you choose to be born into a poor family in a ghetto, black or white, a male or a woman, a despised foreigner, a leper, or with a deformed hand? A Palestinian Jew from Nazareth? Could you just pull yourself up by your bootstraps and make it? What if we lucky Americans and Europeans at this Congress were not born in our countries but rather in violent Honduras, Syria, or Myanmar today? Think about justice as this "original position", putting yourself in someone else's shoes. Then, if you are really honest, you will choose the fairest distributive justice system possible for all, once you dare to imagine that you would get the unequal starting position in life! What good Christian can be against justice knowing this?

Jesus version of fairness in justice is evident in what we call the Golden Rule: Do unto others as you would have them do unto you (Matthew 7:12). How could he say such rules and treat all the downtrodden accordingly and not be for justice?

Another aspect of justice is regarding punishment. Instead of Distributive Justice as we just saw, they call this **Retributive Justice**. Like criminal justice, it asks: what shall we do about wrongdoers, those who violate the Rule of Law, those who have made others suffer? Who shall punish truly evil persons and how? What if the laws themselves are unjust? Can you resist, disobey or break any law in civil disobedience? Wasn't Jesus known as a law-breaker? Was his punishment justifiable? You can see the dilemma about retributive justice.

Although Christians ignore Jesus on this, he does NOT approve of the Law of Retaliation or Lex Talionis, an ancient principle found as early as the Hammurabic Code, from the Babylonian god of justice. Jesus says clearly that you have heard of "an eye for an eye and a tooth for a tooth, but I say turn the other cheek" (Matthew 5:38-42). If someone steals your coat, give him your shirt as well and do not sue him or demand it back. (Luke 6:29). Jesus is not for reciprocal punishment as retributive justice as we see, like: executing drug users less more become drug users, or imprisoning and killing a certain ethnic group in their own homeland, or ignoring drowning "boat people" seeking refuge, or imprisoning attempted-immigrants to make them learn a lesson, or make them an example for deterrence.

Instead, Jesus supports justice that makes amends, and restores peace by forgiveness and by healing instead of punishing. This is what is called *restorative justice*. If you make a mess, yes, you will have to help clean it up, not so much as punishment as restoration. There's a difference. Jesus' teaching and practice indicates He is more attuned to Restorative Justice than Retributive Justice. Jesus' relationship with sinners and wrongdoers, even the wealthy, like Zacchaeus, restores them to society, heals them from their evil ways, and results in them "paying back" voluntarily 4 times more than what they caused in harm. Restorative justice is like conversion, i.e. personal or social change rather than punishment.

None of us can "opt out" of the struggle for justice, and pretend we don't live on planet Earth. All of us share in the injustices and evils that are sadly part of this sinful reality. Jesus seems to uphold an obligation to do something, whenever we do it for the least of our brothers and sisters (Matthew 24: 40).

There are many more concepts of justice that we cannot share today. But the kind of justice Jesus is for is not based on merits or retribution, but is primarily **fairness in distribution and restorative**. And as great as justice is, Jesus always pushes us onward toward another virtue that is even greater. As Thomas Aquinas wrote: " of all the virtues which relate to our neighbor, mercy is the greatest" So then, Jesus is not only for justice but also for mercy.

6. JESUS FOR PEACE:

I will never forget how inspired I was when I first read Pope Paul VI's World Day of Peace Message on January 1, 1972, titled *If You Want Peace, Work for Justice*. In it, Paul VI united Peace with

Justice in a way that we all now realize is essential.

Personally, I have devoted a lot of my ministry to justice and peace and still do. I worked full time for justice and peace organizations, including Catholic justice and peace offices. I was once the Justice & Peace Promoter in my province. I learned organizing skills and founded non-profit organizations for human rights struggles. I went straight into war-torn countries like Nicaragua and El Salvador as a missionary. I have marched for peace and justice causes most of my life, even ending up getting arrested at non-violent protests. I tried to preach Christianity on the frontiers in places like communist Cuba. Some of my own family accuse me of being a revolutionary Christian, though I wish it sounded more prophetic. In light of Pope Paul VI's message, I wanted to apply the principle: if we want peace, we have to work for justice. And of course, that principle is still very true today.

But lately, my thoughts turn more to Peace than to Justice, and how much I have neglected Peace work. Peace seems to have been left "in the back seat" while we are so busy working on what we think are the more important social justice issues! As if Pope Paul had meant, "forget about Peace; Justice is what we need first". Without gettting competitive about it, I think Justice and Peace ministry today is sorely lacking in giving proper attention to Peace.

There have been 51 World Day of Peace messages by the popes. But it does not seem to me that Peace and non-violence are seen as core values of Catholics and the other Christians. It is doubtful that non-Christians of the world think of Christianity as a peace religion. Nor do they see Jesus as a pacifist, despite all the evidence. The Christians do not appear to lead the peace movement.

There is a Big Lie today that blurs the truth about Peace. Governments rename their soldiers Peacekeepers. The Nobel Peace Prize is awarded to lovely individuals like Barack Obama and Aung San Suu Kyi, although they haven't done anything significant to work for peace or non-violence. We depict pacifists and war protesters as hippies or communists.

The world has never been so armed to the teeth, so dangerously violent, yet you hear almost not a word regarding peace and non-violence from preachers. With several simultaneous wars going on, there seems to be no peace movement in our countries. The only word we get is from Pax Christi and the Pope on World Day of Peace. So, if you think Justice is unpopular, I daresay Peace is even moreso, even among us Dominicans.

I have another version of Paul VI's slogan, which is equally true: "If you want justice, work for peace". How are justice advocates going to achieve any social change in the middle of war? One cannot even do Charity work, except in refugee camps, as long as war continues. Why try to build a school or a clinic which will be destroyed tomorrow? How can we achieve any restorative or distributive justice, defend any human rights, reestablish a free press and just court system--while killing continues and the bombs fly overhead? If you want justice, stop the war so we can get some.

It is worse. Christians have justified war and justify the use of violence. Our dear saints Augustine and Thomas Aquinas have fooled Christians and the official Church with their Just War Theory, ignoring everything that Jesus said and did. Did he say shoot back or turn the other cheek? Did he say kill or love your enemy? Did he fight back or let them crucify him? Did he even curse them or instead heal the enemy's wound and forgive them. That Jesus is not a pacifist is the biggest Christian lie that we continue to tell. Or at least, the most deafening silence. Jesus was never for war or for the use of violence, and we all know it.

Truth-telling is never easy today, but especially for those who work for peace. Governments and their military will denounce pacifists as naive, because you can't show how to make peace. But there is nothing more naive than to keep thinking that war works. It doesn't. It should be outlawed, so that we can work on justice issues. In fact, killing the enemy seems to indicate failure of governments and militaries in coming up with anything other than annihilating the problem at hand. So peace is accused of being impractical, but violence isn't? After they tire of their war games, having destroyed all the people, environment and civilization, but won't admit that the whole thing was a failure, these false peacemakers finally come to their senses, sign a peace accords with no victors, then call for a Truth and Reconciliation Commission to be established, obliging the true peacemakers to try and put things back together. Too late they say unite the destroyed people and nation, get on with rebuilding a just society, attempt to heal those raped and traumatized. Thousands of deaths later, thousands of refugees, after they have bombed the hell out of everything, killing more civilians than soldiers (but rarely the rulers who direct the wars from far away). Yet they tell us war is necessary because peace and non-violence doesn't work. Well, it is obvious that war doesn't work either. It is a failure for solving problems and establishing justice and they know it. It is a Big Lie. It's simply more arms production and big sales profits for military-industrial corporations.

We know in our hearts that Jesus is for peace. Love of enemy is the hardest teaching He gives us. Like our work for justice it is scary. But we ought not neglect the challenge of working for peace, studying how to build a more peaceful world, and how to communicate non-violently. Christ is our Peace (Ephesians 2:17) so let us make every effort to do what leads to peace (Romans 14:19).

7. JESUS CARES FOR CREATION:

After hearing the presentations on the Care of Creation by Sister Lissie and Fr. Aristide, and knowing that my presentation was aleady too long, I cut this section of my paper which was about how Jesus not only is for justice and for peace but also loves and Cares for Creation!

8. CONCLUSION:

In conclusion, let us be clear about *WHY* we are working for justice and peace: Jesus, God-with-us, who is our first *WHY*. Jesus, who is for justice as fairness for the poor and the afflicted, and whose justice restore rather than condemns, by forgiveness and mercy not retribution and vengeance. Jesus, who is our Peace and who rejects violence while loving his enemies, is our *WHY*. Jesus who loves the birds of the air and the lilies of the fields and recycles left over bread. This Jesus is *WHY* we are working for justice and peace first and foremost. May He guide and protect all Dominicans in this exciting, prophetic mission of working for a more just and peaceful and sustainable world, working joyfully in His reign already begun on planet Earth.

CLOSING STATEMENT
Ruth Anne Henderson, op

I have been asked by the International Council to present a final impression of this Congress, on the theme, "Our Future: Justice, Peace and Care of Creation". In due course we will all have a copy of the resolutions proposed by the various Commissions and adopted by the voting assembly. Here, let us look at some questions that our time here will help us to answer.

1. *What were the objectives of the Congress?*
   - to experience fraternity across nations and across cultures through our direct daily contact and interaction;
   - to find space for silence and for personal prayer: this was achieved by the possibility of Adoration every morning in the chapel, before the Blessed Sacrament;
   - to foster, not uniformity, but unity: we are very different in so many ways, but we are one in our being Dominicans.

2. *What positive aspects, in particular, emerged?*

    - the presence of many friars, including a number of members of the Curia Generalizia: the Master of the Order, finding a space for us despite being currently involved in the Synod on Youth; his Vicar, Br Miguel Ángel Del Río; the Socius for the Apostolic Life, Br Orlando Rueda Acevedo; the Socius for Fraternal Life and Formation, Br Vivian Boland; and many more. There were also many Promoters from various Provinces around the world, who never dominated our discussions nor imposed their points of view, but listened to us and were unfailingly supportive;
    - the confirmation that communication, whether direct or digital, is fundamental to everything we do or hope to do;
    - an increased awareness of our place as lay Dominicans in the Order of Preachers;
    - fruitful, peaceful discussion in the Commissions: we may sometimes have disagreed, but always in a climate of fraternal exchange and collaboration.

3. *What new objectives have emerged?*

    - the need for more regular and more open communication between fraternities, Provinces, countries and regions;
    - the need for greater uniformity in formation: Hectór Marquéz, for example, told us that, on his visits within his own region, it became apparent that some have little or no formation while others are too rigid and too severe, and this is true worldwide;
    - the need to find a balance between extreme, excessive clericalism in some countries and excessive secularism in others.

4. *What do we need to clarify?*

   - the distinction between the Rule and "regulations", between the essential guidelines for all lay Dominicans and an exaggerated rigidity that is contrary to the spirit of St Dominic himself, who insisted that failure to observe the Rule is, yes, a flaw, but not a sin;

   - the financial situation: Klaus Bornewasser, the ICLDF treasurer, tells us that if even one third of Provinces paid the fixed contribution regularly (€1.50 per person per annum), the Congress could be held free of charge for all delegates.

5. *What problems emerged?*

   - above all, the "Tower of Babel" effect: we speak many languages, and what seems clear in one language may not be so in another; we did not have the anticipated full team of interpreters and several people stepped in to fill the gaps. And of course, there are "false friends": words that resemble each other from one language to another, but in fact have different meanings. All this demands vigilance, and the collaboration of people whose language skills allow them to solve at least some of these problems.

6. *What about the immediate future?*

   - in the next few weeks there will be an opportunity to participate in online, anonymous evaluation of this Congress;

   - there will also be a complete online list of participants: name and surname, country, gender, status (religious or lay), with email addresses and telephone numbers.

7. *And finally, our thanks:*

   - to the Dominican Family in Portugal, and especially to Cristina Busto and Gabriel Silva, for doing so much to make everything run smoothly;

- to the Sisters in Fátima;
- to the hotel staff for their cordiality, patience and efficiency;
- to the interpreters, those invisible angels;
- to all those who animated the liturgy in various ways;
- to the members of the ICLDF, Belen Tangco, Hectór Marquéz, Joe Komadina, Klaus Bornewasser, Felix Foko;
- to the celebrants and preachers;
- to the speakers – a special mention here to the only lay speaker, my fellow-Scot Duncan MacLaren;
- to the many friars who took part;
- to digital Superman Edoardo Mattei;
- to the two former Promoters General who were with us, Br Jerry Stookey and Br David Kammler;
- and of course to our current, greatly loved and respected Promoter General, Br Rui Carlos Antunes e Almeida Lopes, for his tireless work with us and for us.

Thank you, and God bless you all.

INDICE

Made in the USA
Middletown, DE
19 February 2020